Hope Matters

Churchless Sermons in the
Time of the Coronavirus

Andrew Taylor-Troutman

Parson's Porch Books

Hope Matters: Churchless Sermons in the Time of the Coronavirus

ISBN: Softcover 978-1-951472-97-9

Copyright © 2021 by Andrew Taylor-Troutman

Parson's Porch Books is an imprint of Parson's Porch *&* Company (PP*&*C) in Cleveland, Tennessee. PP*&*C is an innovative organization which raises money by publishing books of noted authors, representing all genres. Its face and voice is **David Russell Tullock** (dtullock@parsonsporch.com).

Parson's Porch *&* Company *turns books into bread & milk* by sharing its profits with the poor.

www.parsonsporch.com

Hope Matters

For Ginny

With gratitude for all your support. We can do hard things. And we have fun along the way.

love you dancing free
spin grin to the melody
love you dizzy me

Endorsement

What a beautiful collection of recollections this has turned out to be. As I began reading, I was slightly concerned that *Hope Matters* would dredge up all the sadness and fear of the recent past — living through a pandemic, facing the political and social challenges of 2020, witnessing the death of George Floyd and then moving into a new year that started with an insurrection. Instead, I found each chapter to be enriching and, though sometimes a sad reminder of the many despairing moments of 2020, filled with hope and inspiration. This book calls us to be our better selves and to examine the ways in which we have been part of a system that has disadvantaged so many of our fellow Americans.

In its own gracious and unassuming way, the narration of *Hope Matters* reminds us that we can do hard things, that kindness and compassion are sometimes the only gifts worth giving, and that we will get through this together. I thought 2020 was a year that would best be forgotten. Instead, Andrew presents a collection of weekly editorials that weave together a year that brought out the very best in so many of us in bold and meaningful ways. In the end, it is clear that hope really does matter.

Karen Howard
Chatham County Commissioner

Grateful

100% of my profits from the sale of *Hope Matters* will be donated to the food assistance programs provided by the Farm at Penny Lane and Chapel in the Pines Presbyterian Church. The goal of this partnership is that no person should go hungry in Chatham County, North Carolina.

Each chapter originally appeared in the *Chatham News + Record*, and I'm grateful to publisher and editor Bill Horner. As I tell him, it is a grace to be read.

I also thank Paul Isom for all his help. He graciously edited each week's editorial and contributed the foreword. We share a love of words and a commitment to faith in action. In addition, Paul and I have sat through many a committee meeting together and walked several rounds of disc golf. I am grateful to be his pastor and friend.

Contents

Foreword

We were mired in the depths of the COVID-19 pandemic when my friend and pastor, Andrew Taylor-Troutman, asked me to edit his weekly columns. It was August 2020. On Facebook, people were still debating the need to wear masks. My employer, North Carolina State University, had recently sent me back into the classroom — then changed its mind two weeks later.

Clearly, there was a lot we still didn't know about the virus as it continued to upend our lives.

As a member of the church Andrew leads, Chapel in the Pines Presbyterian, I was usually on the receiving end of his gifts. I was more than happy to offer him my journalism skills, honed in the newsroom and now preached to a congregation of college students. It was nice to be giving something to him for a change!

But, as it turned out, what I gained through editing Andrew's observations and insights far outweighed what I contributed.

As you'll see in these pages, Andrew shares his experiences navigating the pandemic and other challenges with a seminarian's mind, a poet's voice and a disciple's heart.

As the COVID-19 pandemic fades into history, Andrew's words will help us remember what we went through. In that way, this book documents the way our lives were turned upside down, something future generations may find curious or hard to believe.

But more than that, Andrew offers constructive, grounded and loving ways to respond, react and move forward as parents, spouses, children or neighbors, no matter the challenges we face.

Paul Isom

Introduction:
Books Turned into Bread and Milk

This book compiles a full year of my editorials for a local newspaper, the *Chatham News + Record*. It begins with the first week of the COVID-19 pandemic in my community.

I think of my weekly editorials as "churchless sermons," a phrase borrowed from writer David James Duncan. I write as a Christian pastor, but neither exclusively nor specifically for a church audience. I wish to invite readers — including those from different religions and philosophies — to work together for his community's common good and its shared well-being. Without proselytizing or seeking to convert anyone to Christianity, my goal is to inspire more of us to do justice and love kindness (Micah 6:8) by loving our neighbors (Leviticus 19:18; Mark 12:31).

In appealing to a wide community of readers, I build many of my columns from the foundational idea that all of us should care for the most vulnerable: people in need of food, shelter and attention. I believe this call to action can unite us. I found a publisher who feels the same.

Parson's Porch & Company was founded in 2004 "with the sole purpose of helping people to have enough." Every week, Parson's Porch delivers groceries to places that give food to families. I love its motto: "A book publisher turning books into bread and milk." All of this publisher's proceeds from the sale of my book will support food assistance programs.

Likewise, I will donate 100% of my profits to my church's partnership with a local nonprofit called the Farm at Penny Lane. Our programs include a food pantry, meal delivery service and community garden. We provide healthy, free food. With the support of other organizations in our community, our goal is that no person should go hungry in Chatham County, North Carolina.

My book's title, *Hope Matters*, is a nod to the Parson's Porch series "Sermon Matters" — collections written by pastors I admire like Chris Currie and the late Steve Montgomery.

For me, hope matters because it can help us endure crises with grace under duress. The COVID-19 pandemic has been a terrible crisis, yet I hope people of good faith will continue to work together across political and religious differences to support people in need. This not only matters to individuals but can create unity, harmony and good will — qualities that our body politic hungers for.

I'm grateful for your support. Along with Parson's Porch, you and I have turned this book into bread and milk. Maybe some fresh produce or a warm, nutritious meal. That matters.

Andrew Taylor-Troutman

Churchless Sermons in the Time fo the Coronavirus

Words in the Time of the Coronavirus

March 19, 2020

What a week.

Schools, houses of worship and many businesses have been shut down or gone online. Our lives have been upended.

What can we say at such a time as this?

Theologian Roger Owens recently wrote that people of faith should avoid the two extremes of "catastrophic" and "magical" words. We should not speak of the pandemic as if all is hopeless or as if nothing is wrong.

As we seek the middle of these extremes, we need language that is clear, concise and informative. We need to know the exact symptoms of the coronavirus and the ways the infection is spread. We must know the facts about the grave danger before us.

And we seek words of inspiration. We need poetic language, as Bob Dylan sang, "like it was written in my soul from me to you."

On Monday, after Chatham County Schools switched to online learning, my wife wrote in bright green marker on our family's dry erase board: We Can Do Hard Things.

Those words speak to my soul.

This past week, I have found myself repeating this mantra, whether planning online worship for church, coaching parishioners about how to join a Zoom video conference call, assisting my oldest son with his virtual classroom or pinballing with all three of my young children around our suddenly small house. We can do hard things.

Writing about kids and public schools, I am reminded of the families that depend on the meals served in the school cafeterias. Many families were unable to afford groceries before the pandemic, and we can expect a rise in unemployment as a result of the coronavirus shutdowns. All who are able can donate online to our local food pantries. We can put our money where our mouths are and help families in a time of need. We can do hard things.

We can do hard things. I don't think we can say this mantra enough. Such simple words can inspire us and motivate a call to action.

In hard times, I also want to say that we need to hear gracious words of comfort.

Especially when it is hard to know what to say, I turn to certain soulful poems, like Psalm 46, and let them speak for me: "God is our refuge and strength, a very present help in trouble. Therefore, we will not fear, though the earth be removed, and though the mountains be carried into the midst of the sea."

May you hear a word of hope. We can do hard things.

Faith for the Journey Ahead

March 26, 2020

Not to go all Greek on you, but the word for "faith" in that language is pistis. Occasionally, I meet someone named Faith and, in Greek mythology, Pistis was personified as a type of spirit-fairy. She was one of the first to fly from Pandora's box and — after taking a quick look around at the world as it is — promptly winged her way back to heaven!

Maybe a quick look at our world makes you feel like doing the same.

While I have met a couple of people named Faith, I know far more who claim to have lost their faith. And this was before a global pandemic.

Many of us conceptualize faith as a quantity or a possession — something we either have or not, something we can hold onto or lose. Faith that is conceptualized as a possession leads to what writer Joan Didion called magical thinking: a belief that enough faith will act like fairy dust and — abracadabra! — make all our problems fly away.

It is magical thinking to believe that the coronavirus is going to vanish overnight.

I don't know how long we must endure this global pandemic. But I believe it is healthier to think of faith as a journey; not a static thing to possess, but a winding, rocky path up the mountains and back down into the valleys. You and I may not know what lies around the bend or be able to explain the potholes in the road, but we can take the next step forward. Walking in faith is what Pastor Eugene Peterson called "a long obedience in the same direction."

It can be difficult to keeping going in faith, especially during tragic times. There has already been great suffering in parts of our country and world. Things are going to get worse before they get better. We are going to have to travel a long, hard road.

We need to think of faith not only as a personal journey but as a communal effort. Not a race against one another, but a pilgrimage with a supportive crowd. We don't know how long the pandemic will last. We know we are in this together. At a time when we seem to have only a wing and a prayer, walking in faith means doing the next right thing, however simple and insignificant it might seem at the time.

Such faith will not make the coronavirus magically disappear. Faith is trusting the next step, even when the end is not in sight.

A Song of Fierce Hope

April 2, 2020

Due to the shelter-in-place restrictions, I am unable to gather with my church family during Holy Week. I lead services online.

I also worship in the woods around my home. There is a choir in the branches. Surrounded by birdsong, I think of poet Emily Dickinson's lines: "'Hope' is the thing with feathers / that perches on the soul."

It is lovely to personify hope as a songbird. But this bird is tougher than you might suspect. Dickinson wrote of "the Little Bird that kept so many warm." Hope is more than a lovely thought or flight of fancy.

Dickinson wrote this poem in 1862 after it had become clear that the Civil War was not ending anytime soon, and many more people were going to suffer and die — not unlike our time in the coronavirus.

How can we sing a song of hope?

The Easter story flies from the celebration of Palm Sunday to the tragedy of Good Friday. Christians have long walked the Via Dolorosa — the way of suffering and sorrow — to the cross. Every year, people of faith around the world remember that it gets worse before it gets better.

But this year, instead of the metaphor of walking through the valley of the shadow of death, we need to imagine ourselves as a whimbrel — a seabird that can fly through a hurricane!

People of faith have endured storms before. By the time of Jesus, the people of Israel had suffered under the hurricane of foreign occupation for almost 600 years: First by the Babylonians, then the Persians, the Greeks and finally the Romans. Certain regimes were better than others, but the bottom line was that Israel suffered under foreign rule.

The prophets envisioned a coming messiah who would establish a new kingdom on Earth. They found strength for the present in their hope for what was to come: "'For I know the plans I have for you,' says the LORD, 'plans for welfare and not for evil, to give you a future and a hope.'" Jeremiah 29:11 and other prophetic texts are poems of fierce hope.

On the one hand, Americans cannot relate to such brutal occupations. We live in a democracy, a society that enjoys freedoms the ancient world could not have even imagined.

But COVID-19 has stripped away any illusion that we are in control. For all of our technological innovation and medical prowess, we realize that we are at the mercy of forces beyond our powers. The future has always been beyond our ken. We are now keenly aware of this reality.

Hope is a thing with feathers … flying into the hurricane! Let us sing into the storm! Let us trust that there will be clearer skies and brighter days ahead. Trust that, one day, we will flock together again to sing hymns of gratitude. And what a morning that we will be.

What Is a "Good" Explanation for the Coronavirus?

April 9, 2020

The biblical story of creation in the opening chapter of the Book of Genesis is neither a scientific essay nor a proof text. It is a poem — a hymn to the goodness of God. Genesis states that God pronounced creation "good" because God is good and, out of that generosity, willed all that is into being.

With that in mind, what the heck happened? Why are things not good?

It is tragic enough to endure the coronavirus outbreak in New York City. Imagine a refugee camp or a prison. "Why?" is a question that comes to mind.

What, then, is a "good" explanation for the coronavirus?

You and I both know that, in the aftermath of any tragedy, the usual suspects trot out their "explanations" involving God's punishment and the so-called End Times. They might cite isolated Bible verses.

Yet, as biblical scholar N.T. Wright recently claimed in Time magazine, "Christianity offers no answers about the coronavirus." The article is more nuanced than this bombastic headline. Wright claims Christians cannot explain suffering — it is our calling not to explain it! Not knowing how to explain tragedy is deeply biblical. This is called lament.

The Bible's rich history of lament is primarily found in the Psalms. Questions — such as "Why, God?" and "How long, O Lord?" — are left unanswered. They hang in the air on purpose. And why is that?

Last Friday, followers of Jesus read the account of the crucifixion. As Jesus hung on the cross, he let the question hang in the air: "My

God, my God, why have you forsaken me?" The Gospels offer no immediate answer to his question. That is a lament.

We refer to the Friday before Easter as "good" not because Jesus explained suffering. We believe he conquered death. His death and resurrection embody our belief that, when all is said and done, there is nothing in life or death that can separate us from the love of God. Love is ultimately the only answer.

I know it is tempting to look for an answer, to rationalize or explain. If we know why the coronavirus happened, then we can lay the blame on someone else — like China.

But pointing fingers is not an answer.

Those heartfelt prayers in Psalms are meant to bring us together. When we ask the questions together, we wait together. We hope together.

Every year during the Good Friday service, the most moving moment for me is a question sung in the African American spiritual, "Were you there when they crucified my Lord?" We worship together. And that is good.

The Truth of the Daoine Sidhe

April 23, 2020

Though I will remember this year for the COVID-19 outbreak, it was also the time of the daoine sidhe. Pronounced "down she," the legend dates to ancient Ireland. My children know them as the little people of peace who live in the woods behind our neighborhood. They make their homes in the small plants growing beside our creek.

The daoine sidhe are our friends.

I have told my children that the daoine sidhe are small and quick, able to disappear without a trace despite the best efforts of a child to sneak up on them. But kids can write questions in the smooth dirt beside the creek. The daoine sidhe respond the next day with answers scrawled on the backs of large leaves, smooth stones and flat pieces of bark. It's like Santa filling their stockings when they are asleep — except the daoine sidhe are here all year long!

Here are some of my children's questions and the little people's answers:

What do you eat? Nuts and berries.

Do you have pets? Bumblebees.

Do you like Christmas? Yes, especially the presents.

My children have left gifts of soft feathers and bright leaves and later discovered pebbles stacked in a small tower and a pile of red berries. Although I prohibited them from eating the offering from the daoine sidhe, they still built the little people a tiny obstacle course of twigs for their enjoyment.

After tucking them in their beds at night, I've told my kids that the daoine sidhe were once the size of young boys and girls. They lived among the rest of us, but they had decided to shrink and retreat into the woods because of the cruelty and callousness of those who did not treat the plants and animals of the forests and creeks with respect and kindness.

All of us are trying to cope with the coronavirus. No one is to blame. But we humans are the cause of extinction, pollution and environmental degradation. Over the course of my life, I've heard scientists, politicians and environmentalists call with increasing urgency for our society to address climate change. The facts have been clear about the imminent global disaster. The signs are all around us.

But it took a global pandemic and economic shutdown to decrease our carbon output.

The virus has been devastating to our way of life. Yet, smog has lifted from skylines from Los Angeles to New Delhi. Streams and rivers now run clearer and cleaner. Birds can once again be heard from fire escapes from Manhattan to Beijing.

Will we realize that we can choose to protect our planet rather than be forced to change by a deadly disease? The science is clear, but the threat is often rationalized, politicized or ignored. In addition to the facts, we need stories — deep truths that move our hearts.

My kids think of the daoine sidhe as their friends. My hope is that they learn to slow down and wonder about the world around them. If my children learn to respect and value the woods and creeks as homes for other creatures, they are more likely to grow up to respect and value the rest of the natural world.

Transformation can start with small things. That is the truth.

Words Matter: Part 1

April 30, 2020

I keep hearing that we are at war with the coronavirus.

Though I have never experienced a life-threatening disease, I do know the flu can feel like an invasive force. I am also familiar with phrases like, "she battled cancer," or, "he fought the disease to the end."

I believe that doctors, surgeons, nurses and health care workers are heroes in every sense of the word. They are "in the trenches" and "on the front lines." They put their own lives at risk.

I also understand that people relate the war metaphor to the coronavirus as a means to "rally the troops." Some people treat social distancing and mask-wearing with cavalier attitudes, and this will cost lives. To speak of our war with the coronavirus is an effort to instill the deadly seriousness of this crisis.

But despite all of these reasons, language of war is problematic.

During the coronavirus pandemic, we have been asked to forgo certain personal freedoms for the greater good. As shelter-in-place orders have been instituted "to combat" the spread of the coronavirus, other arguments counter that our individual rights are "under attack."

We may begin by thinking that our enemy is a virus. But when our language becomes adversarial, we forget that we are on the same team. The poet Sherman Alexie recently offered this diagnosis for our times: "Maybe the true pandemic is the loss of a shared and common decency."

It is no secret that our society was divided along political lines before the coronavirus. When we apply the language of war in the context of that partisanship, I fear that we may even start to see one another as enemies. Such conflict among ourselves is especially dangerous at this time. We need to work together in order to contain and, ultimately, survive such a highly infectious disease. We need to care for one another.

Words create worlds. The way we speak shares a vision of who we are and where we want to go from here. We need language that encourages us to relate to one another; a way of communicating that encourages interconnectedness and mutual support. Instead of promoting division and violence, we need a metaphor that offers healing through unity.

Thankfully, such a metaphor is readily available to us. In fact, we have had such language for a long time. As our society has been sickened with a new disease, it may be that ancient wisdom is part of the cure that heals us: "The body is one and has many members, and all the members of the body, though many, are one body."

We are not at war; we are one body.

Words Matter: Part 2

May 7, 2020

Words create worlds. Our choice of language speaks volumes about how we imagine our predicaments, our future and ourselves. I believe it is problematic to speak of the coronavirus as if fighting a war. Instead of the language of combat or battle, there is an alternative that comes from ancient wisdom.

We are not at war; we are one body.

"The body is one and has many members, and all the members of the body, though many, are one body."

This quotation is from the New Testament (1 Corinthians 12:12). Yet, the image is even older and finds parallels in our cultures. The Rigveda, Hinduism's most ancient scripture, envisioned the body as a metaphor for human community in 1500 BCE. The idea that we are all connected and reliant upon one another has stood the test of time.

As a result of the pandemic, many people have lost loved ones. Many more face financial hardship from loss of employment or income. How could this image of humanity as one body change how we respond to such pain and suffering? 1 Corinthians 12:25–26 offers the following:

"The members may have the same care for one another. If one member suffers, all suffer together."

We do not all suffer equally or in the same ways. Thinking of others as part of our one body affords us the opportunity to imagine their pain. This is called empathy — putting yourself in someone else's shoes.

Empathy begins with our individual experience. We are each aware of our own personal health, whether it is good or bad, and no one is immune to suffering. We can draw on this experience as we imagine what it is like to be someone else.

Other than our own pain, we are most aware of the suffering of those who are closest to us. My wife and I have three young children. In my nuclear family, I know the truth that, if one person suffers, then we all suffer.

But the bodily and spiritual connections are not as readily apparent with people in China, Seattle or even in my own neighborhood. Having empathy for people outside my immediate relatives as members of the same human family requires a leap of imagination.

In response to someone else's tragic news, we might sigh, "Oh, I can't even imagine." While that sentiment is well-intentioned, we must try to empathize.

Think of a grandfather who no longer gets to hold his only grandchild. Picture a widow watching YouTube videos of quarantined Italians singing across darkened city streets instead of singing in her church choir. Imagine a single father typing an e-mail to his boss filled with grammatical mistakes because he was simultaneously trying to recall his long-lost geometry skills in order to help his daughter with her schoolwork. Or a hairdresser waking up with a dry cough and, kissing her toddler on top of his head, having to decide whether or not to miss a day's wages.

We must try to imagine. Personalizing the suffering inspires us to embody care for one another. How we speak about this pandemic is crucial because words inform our actions, and actions display our values. This, too, is ancient wisdom: "Do unto others what you would have them do unto you."

In light of this Golden Rule, let us not say that we are at war with the coronavirus. Let us be one body helping one another to heal.

Bless Your Heart

May 14, 2020

During this global health crisis, fear abounds. Fear for our health, fear for our economy, fear of the unknown.

Perhaps a mantra or verse of sacred scripture helps you "keep calm and carry on," as the slogan goes. You can also find hope in the actions and attitudes of folks around you. People do "small things with great love" (Mother Teresa).

I was in the checkout line at the grocery store which, these days, involves masks, gloves and social distancing. You don't trust a sneeze. Though there is no toilet paper, there's anxiety on every aisle.

Yet, the young clerk at the register was calm and collected. Her millennial generation is often maligned, but I watched her load an elderly man's groceries into his cart. Then, she smiled as she wished him a "blessed day."

"Bless you," the man replied.

A word about this word, bless. I grew up in the South, so I know that the phrase "bless your heart" may be used as an excuse to say whatever god-awful thing you want about another person.

On the other hand, we count our blessings and are grateful for them. To be blessed often means to receive things such as shelter, food, health. Blessing entails happiness, grace, favor.

Blessing can also refer to our act of giving. The old German root of "bless" is the same as "blood," which referred to animal sacrifices on an altar. I'm not interested in such offerings. But we can bless others with our loving sacrifices.

Thinking of that man in the grocery store, I know that many of our elders are tucked out of sight in assisted living facilities. The virus has devastated many of these communities. These men and women had lived through wars, stock market crashes and diseases. Many had survived both global and personal tragedies. And now many have suffered and died alone.

There are healthcare workers who risk their own lives in order to care for these elders. One nurse held a friend's mother in her arms as the dying woman breathed her last. When my friend called to express his gratitude, this nurse replied, "It was a blessing." How could such a terrible tragedy be a blessing?

Such a blessing is about compassion — a word that means to suffer with. To suffer with another person is to offer the gift of love in action. Perhaps a loving sacrifice gives a blessing that lives even after your light has departed from this world. What I know is that, even though fear abounds in this pandemic, people do small things with great love. Bless their brave hearts.

Let's Rocket Past Normal

May 21, 2020

The coronavirus pandemic has brought physical, economic and emotional suffering. No one knows what the future holds. Greater hardships and more tragedies may be yet to come. We do not even know if the end is in sight.

I want to return to a level of normalcy, meaning I want to know what to expect.

But let's not use the phrase "new normal." I think we can do much better.

Please understand that I do not wish to diminish or dismiss the tragedies that have occurred as a result of COVID-19. But not everything is worse than before.

Blue skies are now seen over cities for the first time in decades. Birdsong can once again be heard in factory towns. Rivers and oceans are running clearer and cleaner. Carbon emissions are lower in countries around the world.

Seeking distance from crowds, more people are retreating to wild places for solitude and discovering their beauty.

People are not only connecting to the natural world but to one another as well. The irony of social distancing is that the separation has caused many people to pick up a phone and call extended family members and neighbors just to check in.

For the first time since we moved to our neighborhood in 2018, people are spending evenings on their front porches and talking to one another from a safe distance. Less television is watched, more laughter is heard.

Whereas "normal" just a few months ago would have included bitter partisan politics, today the majority of us recognize the sacrifice necessary to care for the common good. We are overwhelmingly supportive of our essential employees. Every evening, bells can be heard on our block and in the distance as we solemnly salute our heroic health care workers.

Such things are not normal. They put a smile on our faces, send shivers down our spines and bring tears to our eyes.

Thinking of heroes, perhaps you know the story of the Apollo 13 lunar module. When the oxygen tank failed, the fear arose that the spaceship would not return safely to Earth. Gene Kranz, the lead flight director, overheard fellow NASA employees fearing that this could be the worst disaster in the organization's history. But Kranz responded:

"With all due respect, I believe this is going to be our finest hour."

We also have an incredible opportunity. Let's be extraordinary.

Let's rocket past "normal."

What Is Essential about Church?

May 28, 2020

Even with the recent decision by the North Carolina Supreme Court to allow religious communities to gather for worship, the governing board of elected lay leaders at my church voted unanimously to continue the suspension of our in-person gatherings, including Sunday-morning worship. As the pastor, I fully support this decision. According to health officials, Saturday, May 23, marked the highest one-day increase of COVID-19 cases in our state.

My heart goes out to all people of faith who long to return to their houses of worship. But in light of recent controversy about "reopening" churches, it is important to say that no community of faith has ever been "closed" due to the coronavirus.

Many groups have shifted to online gatherings. But what exactly is "essential" about worship? What makes worship indispensable and life-giving? What is the core, crux, essence?

As a Christian, I believe it is the Holy Spirit that instructs our hearts and minds (John 14:26), prompts us to prayer and praise (Romans 8:26), and gives us the "peace that surpasses all understanding" (Philippians 4:7). In any time and place, no matter the trials and tribulations, we can "abound in hope" (Romans 15:13).

And we do not have to gather in a church building to experience the gifts of the Holy Spirit.

That said, I recognize that there is no online form of worship that is the same as the in-person experience of being together in church. But in response to the recent state Supreme Court decision, my overriding concern is not with individual rights but communal responsibilities.

I consider individual rights, including the First Amendment, to be of great importance. And yet, as a Christian, I recognize that my ultimate source of freedom is in Christ (Galatians 5:1) and his commandment to love others. Jesus told us what was essential in John 13:35: "Everyone will know that you are my disciples if you love one another."

This love (agape) is expressed by voluntarily sacrificing certain things for the common cause. As people of faith and citizens of humanity, we must act out of loving concern for those most vulnerable and at higher risk in our community as well as those brave women and men who sacrifice their own well-being in order to care for the sick. We must choose to forgo the right to gather in person, for we have a responsibility to obey the higher law of love.

This greater responsibility is also an opportunity to demonstrate the value of our faith to the larger community. I believe the Holy Spirit inspires us every day of the week, and not only on Sundays. Writing about the effects of the Holy Spirit on people, an ancient writer named Paul of Tarsus named nine virtues as the Fruit of the Spirit: love, joy, peace, patience, kindness, gentleness, faithfulness, generosity and self-control. Paul added, "There is no law against such things" (Galatians 5:22–23).

While respecting the shelter-in-place orders during the coronavirus pandemic, people of faith have used their energy, intelligence and imagination to bear the Fruit of the Spirit in new and creative ways. Our congregation is donating money to local restaurants. These businesses buy fresh, local ingredients from farmers, then create nutritious meals that a nonprofit organization delivers to adults with severe mental illness.

Through such creative partnerships, people of faith have the opportunity to demonstrate to the public what is essential about faith communities — it's not the buildings where we gather but the love that we share with the world.

A Prayer for Courage

June 4, 2020

"God grant me the serenity to accept the things I cannot change."

Many readers will recognize the opening line of The Serenity Prayer. It is often recited at the close of a 12-step meeting such as Alcoholic Anonymous.

I have been praying, however, in light of the news of recent violence against African Americans and other people of color. I've focused on the second part of this prayer, which is perhaps not as well known:

"God grant me courage to change the things I can."

Today, I and other white Americans do not have to accept the racially motivated violence against our fellow citizens. We do not have to accept that a young Black man can be killed for jogging in a neighborhood. We do not have to accept that a defenseless Black man can be pinned to the ground by his neck with the knee of a police officer until he dies. We do not have to accept that other white police officers would stand by and watch as this Black man pleaded, "I can't breathe."

We *can* change such things! But we will need the courage to change ourselves.

America has a tragic history of racism that predates the founding of our country. Racism was institutionalized in the Constitution, then legislated in slavery and segregation. The violence against Black people today demonstrates that racism persists in our 21st century society.

Yet another truth is that too many white Americans, though perhaps sympathetic to suffering, have acted as though we are unable to change such things. Too many of us have accepted a false sense of serenity.

Of course, few white Americans actually perpetuate deadly violence against anyone. But we white people must listen to Black and Brown people's descriptions of the double standards, the abuse and the fear that is part of the reality of being a racial minority in this country. For example, Black men tell stories of the first time a police officer pulled a gun on them. So many have such stories to tell!

Instead of listening, however, many Americans are turning a deaf ear to the cries for justice because isolated acts of vandalism and violence have been part of a few, largely peaceful protests.

Rev. Dr. Martin Luther King Jr. said, "Riot is the language of the unheard." We must hear the truth behind the frustration and anger. Listening to learn takes a specific kind of courage.

Step No. 4 of the recovery program for addicts is "to make a searching and fearless moral inventory of ourselves." It is time for white Americans to take this step toward recovery. Addictions cause people to make excuses in order to justify themselves. In this case, I often hear people say that they will not apologize for being white. That is not the point.

The point is that racism is *not* a thing of the past. Like an addiction, we remain in the grips of a horrible cycle. Segregation is prevalent in our public schools and private housing sectors. Prisons are filled with people of color. Police violence is disproportionally directed against minorities. To confess that our society is addicted is painful, but confession is also holy.

Once we have admitted the problem, then we can do something about it.

Long ago, a brown-skinned rabbi from Nazareth claimed that the truth shall set us free. May we have the courage to change the things we can so that, one day, our prayer will be answered: "Free at last, Free at last! Thank God almighty we are free at last!"

United by Our Mamas

June 11, 2020

It seems these United States are more divided every day. We have cultural divisions between urban, rural and suburban. We have political divisions. We have gender and racial divisions.

In some corners, the solution is violence. On the one hand, vandalism and arson. On the other, big guns and lots of troops. But if history proves anything, it is that fighting fire with fire makes bigger fires. Or, as was said long ago, those who live by the sword, die by the sword.

Recently, Gen. James Mattis criticized those in these United States who would "divide and conquer" by attempting to appear as aggressive, tough and dominant leaders. Instead, Gen. Mattis maintained that "in union there is strength." Police officers kneeling before protesters. Civilians giving police officers bottles of water. Volunteers gathering at dawn to sweep up broken glass. Most of all, people protesting peacefully — people of different colors wearing masks and lifting their voices as one to decry the violence that has spilled innocent blood.

The protests have been sparked because a man was lynched in our streets. George Floyd begged for his life, yet the cruel and cavalier police officer continued to suffocate him. Near the end, Floyd stopped pleading with his attacker and evoked someone else:

"Mama! Mama, I'm through!"

When Floyd called for his mama, his killers were unmoved. They could not see him as someone's son just like them.

But a bystander called out, "He is a human being!"

We must understand the inherent worth of each person. Even with all of our differences, many of us know that no one loves us like our mama. This reminds me of another dying man who looked down from the cross and saw his mama. That same man commanded us to love one another so that we would be strong and united as one body.

We will never know what George Floyd's mother would have done, for she preceded her son in death by two years. Now, it is up to us to work for justice and be united in our efforts to reform our society. We can finally end the scourge of racism that is America's original and most damning sin.

Protests create change by inspiring reform. At a recent march organized by the student chapter of the NAACP, I saw dozens of young children walking down the street, hand in hand with their siblings, parents, friends and elders. In union there is the strength. Divisions can fall, barriers can disappear, and justice can become reality. For George Floyd, for all the slain Black sons and daughters, for all the people who loved them, may our hands and hearts wield the love that makes the evil forces quail.

May we make our mamas proud.

Grief Matters

June 18, 2020

Psychiatrist Elizabeth Kubler-Ross formatted her five-stage theory of grief after decades of counseling dying patients and their families. After the death of George Floyd, America has witnessed the collective grief of Black people, and the second stage is now prominent — anger.

In seminary, I studied the stages of grief. I also studied the Psalms — a collection of 150 hymns of ancient Israel that express a range of human emotions. The most dramatic example of rage is found in Psalm 137: "Daughter Babylon, doomed to destruction, happy is the one who repays you according to what you have done to us. Happy is the one who seizes your infants and dashes them against the rocks!"

The psalmist uttered this curse after Babylon had destroyed Jerusalem. Many of the Israelites were slaughtered. The survivors were forced into slavery in a foreign land. Psalm 137 represents the pain of a community that had experienced national trauma.

We might anticipate that grief would look more like the opening verse of Psalm 137: "By the rivers of Babylon we sat and wept when we remembered Zion." But anger is just as much a part of grief as wailing. After a death, particularly a violent one, anger is neither misplaced nor inappropriate.

As part of the process, anger needs to be expressed. Not repressed. To deny anger does not make it disappear. The great poet of the Harlem Renaissance, Langston Hughes, provocatively asked: "What happens to a dream deferred? Does it explode?"

This is an explosive time. We can expect protesters to channel their anger in constructive ways which do not lead to violence or damage property. And yet, we must not deny the anger, for this denies the pain.

This denial is the reason that many protesters express frustration with the All Lives Matter movement. Of course, all lives matter. But the current trauma is from the loss of *Black* lives. To fail to recognize this point is to short circuit the process of grief for a community.

Perhaps by saying "all lives matter," certain well-intentioned people may appeal to the acceptance stage of the Kubler-Ross theory. At this fifth stage, mourners find a sense of closure. They are able to move on. Even live into a new dream.

But, as Hughes warned, a dream deferred is a false closure. This is not acceptance but injustice. I am reminded of the words of the prophet Jeremiah, who was alive around the same time that Psalm 137 was written: "Everyone deals falsely. ... They have treated the wound of my people carelessly, saying, 'Peace, peace,' when there is no peace."

Properly understood, the Black Lives Matter movement reflects a recently added stage six of the theory of grief — meaning. This new stage pushes beyond acceptance. To make meaning neither denies pain nor attempts to rationalize it, but rather asserts new purpose in the aftermath of loss.

Making meaning out of the deaths of Black men and women clarifies goals and values. This effort is evidenced by social-justice initiatives for police reform, affordable housing, living wages and universal health care.

To make meaning out of grief is also about claiming one's own inherent self-worth. Tragedy does not make you less of a human being. Neither does the color of your skin.

At a recent Black Lives Matter protest, a young speaker shouted into a megaphone, "Black is beautiful!" She reminded me that Psalm 137 is not the final word in the Old Testament. Thinking about the grief of the Black community, it matters that Song of Songs 1:5 amplifies the same message as the young woman: "I am black and beautiful, O daughters of Jerusalem."

Patience Like a River

June 25, 2020

During this global pandemic, we have witnessed terrible suffering not only by those who are sick and dying but also by those experiencing financial hardship. The number of unemployed Americans has skyrocketed by more than 14 million since the outbreak, from 6.2 million in February to over 20 million by the end of May.

In light of such suffering, I understand the desire to reopen the economy. The coronavirus threatens both our lives and livelihoods.

And yet, the most credible public health officials warn that we will do more harm by rushing to reopen.

Now is a time for patience.

The word "patience" can mean "long-suffering" and brings to mind a certain biblical character. Job was an ancient man who suffered the loss of nearly everything — his loved ones, his wealth, his own health. Tragically, many people can relate.

While many others have suffered more losses, the pandemic has been a difficult time for my little family. My wife and I are trying to manage two churches and three young children.

I'm not tired of waiting to reopen, for waiting is in the best interests of those who are at high risk for infection and those who care for the sick.

I'm just plain tired.

Every night, after reading books to my young sons, I get down on all fours so the 7-year-old and the 4-year-old can jump on my back. I am the horse, and they are the knights!

But lately, I have been moving more slowly. So slowly that, the other night, my older son informed me that I was no longer a horse. Now I was a cow! And my new name was Old Bessie!

Maybe you can't teach an old cow new tricks, but I've summoned enough energy to reexamine this word "patience" in hopes that I might discover a more life-giving perspective. I learned that the Latin root for "patience" was used by the Romans to describe rivers. How might we be patient like a river?

When told to be patient, we may feel like we are stuck and helpless to do anything. This feeling causes weariness, even despair.

Yet, a river is always moving, slowly yet surely changing the land around it. A river always makes a difference, even if it takes a long time.

Especially in trying circumstances, it's hard to see the effects of gradual change. But in six months, a year, a decade from now, what will we see when we look back on this time? Certainly, we will remember the suffering. I hope we will remember the brave women and men who helped to alleviate it.

Will we remember how we were patient? Will we see the difference that we made and the lives that we saved by being slow and steady?

Thinking of the patience of a river, I recall Norman Maclean's beautiful novella, "A River Runs Through It." The father is a fly fisherman and also a Presbyterian pastor. He believed that all good things — trout as well as eternal salvation — "come by grace and do not come easily."

Many of us are tired. We are tired of being tired. But take it from your Old Bessie: A river of patience makes a Grand Canyon of difference.

School's Out Forever

July 9, 2020

In addition to a nod at the rock 'n' roll song by Alice Cooper, my title is hyperbole. I don't really think that schools should be permanently closed.

But with the rise in COVID-19 cases, I do write to raise questions about sending students back this fall.

The American Academy of Pediatrics did recommend reopening schools. The argument is that the risks of children not being in school — loss of socialization, lack of access to secure food sources, increased exposure to domestic strife — outweigh the risk of getting infected with the coronavirus.

But let's notice that mitigating these risk factors is beyond the purpose of schools to educate our children. Why does school have to be the sole service provider for these other essentials?

We are in the midst of a lethal global pandemic. Our schools need more support not only in terms of buildings, curriculums and teachers but also with other community services for children and families. We need to reimagine how we support and care for our children, and we must be willing to make effective changes in these unprecedented times.

Tragically, the coronavirus has revealed a lack of such vision.

From the beginning of the outbreak, elected and appointed officials at local, state and federal levels have spoken of the desire to return to normal. Often, this prioritizes the economy. Perhaps the most extreme example was the lieutenant governor of Texas suggesting that senior citizens should be willing to sacrifice their lives so that people can get back to work.

Now we hear officials at the highest levels of the federal government insisting schools reopen, fully and on time. Do they expect teachers to sacrifice their lives? Cafeteria workers, janitors and school bus drivers? What about our children?

It's important to remember that the coronavirus is "novel," meaning brand new. There have been no long-term studies. While the mortality rates among children are low, we do not know the morbidity rates. We do not know the damaging effects of the virus on our children.

Notice I write "our" children. My wife and I parent three young ones. But any society that does not consider each and every child as its own is a society lacking in moral imagination.

Why would our political leaders be willing to gamble the long-term health of our children for the short-term viability of our economy? What does *that* say about our family values?

I want to be clear that my criticism is levied against the institutions of our society and those who have been charged to lead them. I have only sympathy for everyone who has to make the hard choice about whether or not to send their children to school. My wife and I have to make the best decision for our family. I know that, for other caregivers, there are no options. I do not judge.

My point is that our society could reimagine ways to meet the needs of children without putting large numbers of people at risk for infection. I want a vision of productive change in the face of pandemic and not a misguided attempt to return to normal.

Be Like John and Vote

July 23, 2020

"Be like Mike" is the advertising jingle I remember from my childhood, although I couldn't say for sure whether the marketing was for Gatorade or Nike. Still, every boy I knew shot baskets with his tongue hanging out like the Chicago Bulls Superstar.

Growing up, I learned that Michael Jordan didn't make his high school basketball team. His failure motivated him to work harder. I bought into that lesson, which has proven far more valuable than high-top shoes or sugary sports drinks.

Sports can teach life lessons. But with all due respect to Air Jordan, now is a time for us to "Be like John" — John Lewis. This legendary Civil Rights leader and congressman leaves a legacy of courage and determination.

Lewis also learned from the adversity of his childhood. He grew up as the son of sharecroppers. When strong winds threatened to lift their ramshackle house from its foundation, Lewis and his siblings threw their bodies on the floor. The team effort saved their home.

Today's crises threaten the livelihood of many families. The coronavirus pandemic has wrought financial havoc, unemployment and insecurity. Against these terrible forces, we must come together. The weight of collective action can make a life-saving difference.

John Lewis would have laid down his life so that you and I could lift up our voices. Yet at a time when we need one another, political winds threaten equal opportunities to vote. Polling locations are closed. Restrictive photo identification laws are in effect. The Postal Service has been financially gutted at a time when the mail-in ballot is more important than ever to prevent the risk of exposure to the contagious disease at the polls.

I urge my fellow residents of Chatham County to request your 2020 State Absentee Ballot. Register today so that your paperwork is completed on time. Act now so that you can vote safely.

Perhaps the greatest threat to our democracy is a lack of motivation. Cynicism is also a national pandemic. People claim that individuals cannot make a difference, that common people are powerless against a corrupt system.

John Lewis did not believe that was true. And neither did our Founding Fathers. They charged us to form a more perfect union, meaning that the country was imperfect at its founding, and it is our calling live into our nation's highest ideals of liberty and justice for all. Your vote is not only a right but a responsibility.

While there was breath in him, John Lewis fought for the voting rights of every American. Be like John. Free and fair elections are the moral force of a democracy. Now it is our time to demonstrate our weight at the ballot box so that we the people hold our representatives accountable for their failure to provide courageous, honest leadership in the face of the storm of COVID-19.

We live in challenging, often tragic circumstances, but not every loss is a defeat. Adversity can inspire us to come together as a team.

The Youth Are the Keys

July 30, 2020

In Greek mythology, Daedalus cautioned his beloved son, Icarus, to fly the middle course in order to avoid the ocean's spray below and the sun's heat above. But Icarus flew too high, melting the wax off his feathered wings. The youth fell and drowned in the sea.

The ancients Greeks called this middle course the Golden Mean, the average between excess and deficiency. The Buddha taught the Middle Way as part of the spiritual path. The idea is the same — avoid the extremes.

And yet, as poet Jack Gilbert reminds us, everyone forgets that Icarus still flew.

We need creativity, innovation and boldness to reach new heights. History teaches that, in the name of moderation, people have grounded progress. They've quenched the spirit rather than fanned the flames.

I realize such inflammatory language carries risks. We do not need recklessness.

But I remember Dr. Martin Luther King Jr.'s letter from a jail cell in Birmingham, Alabama. He asserted that the so-called "white moderate" actually did more harm to Blacks than the Ku Klux Klan. In the name of moderation, nothing was done to help people suffering under oppression.

King relied on Black youths, such as John Lewis and other brave men and women in the Student Nonviolent Coordinating Committee, to lead the charge for equal rights.

Then, as now, the younger generations are the keys not only to the future but also to the present. The young women and men who are coming of age today are the leaders of the now.

Youths are natives to modern technological culture. They speak the language. Such technologies are here to stay. The question is, how will they be used?

Granted, certain social media platforms are misused for such terrible things as bullying. But youths also organize for political action via social networking platforms like Facebook, Instagram and Twitter. They are moving the rest of our society forward on key issues.

Until schools were closed due to the coronavirus, there was a mass shooting every single month of our recent graduates' high school careers. In survey after survey, a majority of Americans supported common-sense measures of gun control. Popular legislation, such as limits on the sale of assault rifles, still has been thwarted by conservative and moderate lawmakers.

But teenagers across the country have organized peaceful marches and protests to enact life-saving reform. Many Americans have passionate opinions about their guns. Young people are changing hearts and minds so they might change the laws.

Our youths have seen the rise of carbon dioxide levels every single year of their lives. While there are climate change deniers, the so-called moderate voices have stymied political action.

But youths have acted to break the gridlock. In countries all over the globe, they have gathered in massive rallies to demand action to curb carbon dioxide emissions. They are the most informed generation in history about the dangers of climate change. Quite literally, our young people are out to save the world.

Despite the enormity of such problems like mass shootings and climate change, I have hope. The younger generations are ready to take the keys and get behind the wheel in order to steer us into a better future.

May we even take to the air and soar.

The Signs of Our Times

August 6, 2020

This summer, residents of Pittsboro raised money to display the Black Lives Matter moniker on a billboard on Highway 64. This billboard stands only a few feet away from a massive Confederate flag. The contrasting images brought national media attention to the town.

There has been a less-publicized brouhaha in the residential community where I live in northern Chatham County. The HOA suddenly enforced a rule that restricted yard signs to realtors and security systems. This was intended "to promote and protect the character of the community."

Though this sign restriction had been part of the HOA agreement, it was never strictly upheld until recently. I don't think it is a coincidence that a neighbor made Black Lives Matter signs available for widespread purchase last month.

Denouncing the Black Lives Matter billboard, a gentleman in Pittsboro falsely claimed that BLM stood for "burn, loot and murder." The pushback against signs in my neighborhood is couched in more diplomatic terms. Some have argued that any political statement focuses on our differences at the expense of our commonalities. In a public statement, a board member of the HOA stated that the sign restrictions reflect "the overall intention for the community to be cohesive."

"Cohesive" means "to join together," and the Latin root was originally a medical term in reference to a procedure to heal the body, such as binding a wound. Our body politic is hurting.

But a body is not joined together by denying the injuries to individual members.

The Stars and Bars flag flies next to the BLM billboard on Highway 64. The rubber meets the road here in my neighborhood. I did not place a Black Lives Matter sign in my yard for "virtue signaling" — the desire to publicly demonstrate my political correctness or moral rectitude. The sign "speaks" of my intention to work for justice and equity. Our body politic is hurting, but this is not a metaphor for Black people. Americans have seen the images of Black bodies lying dead in the streets. A desire for unity or cohesion does not prevent us from taking a public stance against atrocities.

Southern Baptist leader Russell Moore, who is not a bleeding-heart liberal, characterized the sign of our times: "One of the great problems that we have in American life across the board is that we don't ultimately believe that we're going to be able to persuade one another of anything. And so, we assume all we can do is push one another into their categories and to speak about them rather than to them."

Moore's words raise this question in my mind: How would I feel if a neighbor flew a Confederate flag from his front porch right next to my BLM yard sign?

I would rather have an honest debate than quietly retreat into our respective homes. Our country's wounds will not be healed by pretending that everything is fine.

An Open Letter to Parents and Caregivers

August 13, 2020

We are starting school in the throes of a pandemic. We have no recipe to follow. You don't need a lecture from me.

What you really need is chocolate!

But, since I am able to serve words to you, I offer an invitation:

Feel all the feels.

The ups and downs. The contradictions, multitudes and paradoxes. The "hues and blues in equal measure," according to singer-songwriter Alanis Morrisette. The beautiful and brutal — the brutiful.

Remind yourself to breathe deeply. Feel all the feels, though emotions may be raw. Cooking begins with raw ingredients.

Alongside this invitation, I would offer two specific hopes.

First, I hope you have compassionate people in your life who will listen to your feelings without judgment. People who will bear witness to your feelings and your story — not try and change your words to fit their own stories. I hope you know at least one person with the gift of attentive listening. Maybe this gracious individual would give chocolate as well.

(Chocolate, by the way, qualifies as a vitamin in a pandemic. I should know. I personally know several doctors!)

The truth is that we cannot change the reality of COVID-19. We cannot resolve the complexity of schooling in this pandemic or fix any family's dilemma with an easy answer. There are lots of raw emotions, but no magic recipes.

But, if we give ourselves permission to feel our feelings and share them openly and honestly with people we trust, we can change the way we see ourselves.

A wise friend shared a modern parable about looking into the mirror and seeing a smudge. You could scrub and polish that glass with every ounce of cleaning spray in your house. Or you could realize that the chocolate stain is actually on your own cheek! Then, you could gently wash your face with a soft loofah sponge and lavender soap.

This brings me to my second hope — you will be gentle with yourself. The problems are complex. The struggle is real. You are doing the best you can. No one knows exactly what to expect. Brutiful things will happen.

Take your chocolate vitamins! I'm rooting for you.

A Call for Better Angels, Not 'Nasty' Women

August 20, 2020

It took all of two minutes for President Donald Trump to call Sen. Kamala Harris "nasty" after the announcement of her candidacy for vice president. Unfortunately, our president has a long history of using such unpresidential language toward women.

It is also true that Trump has appointed women to positions of power: White House counselor Kellyanne Conway; Gina Haspel of the CIA; and, of course, his daughter, Ivanka Trump.

The president's overriding concern explains this apparent contradiction: Whether man or woman, Trump values loyalty above all else. He does not want criticism from his team of leaders. As an example, look no further than Dr. Anthony Fauci whose expert medical opinion has been ignored, even contradicted, by Trump.

Certainly, no one wishes for a personal attack. But it is ancient wisdom that, as iron sharpens iron, so a person who challenges me can make me stronger (Prov 27:17).

The Founding Fathers envisioned the vice president as the runner-up to the national election for the presidency. Imagine a White House coalition between our current president and his runner-up — the same woman he infamously called "nasty" in the 2016 presidential debate!

By the early 19th century, candidates were selecting their own running mates. Yet, President Abraham Lincoln appointed three cabinet members who had previously campaigned against him — his political enemies! As Pulitzer Prize-winning historian Doris Kearns Goodwin put it, Lincoln formed "a team of rivals" because he wanted to examine problems from every angle, factoring in his own weaknesses and mistakes. Lincoln was a self-secure, self-confident leader. Not only could he take criticism, but Lincoln also believed the feedback made him stronger and wiser. That iron sharpened iron.

The ancient Greeks stressed the importance of phronesis, meaning "practical wisdom." This refers to the ability to discern the moral good in daily life — life amid the changes, challenges and complexities. The Greeks were famous for their debates. They believed that arguing with a leader was neither evidence of disdain nor a sign of disloyalty. Political opponents should not be belittled through childish name-calling but engaged in mature conversation. This is still how the best decisions are reached.

In a time of a global pandemic, our democracy needs practical wisdom from people of good will from all sides. Our leaders must come to the table and challenge one another in constructive ways. The goal should not be to tear down the other side but to build up our country. Though he spoke in 1857, no one has put it better than Lincoln:

"We are not enemies, but friends. We must not be enemies. Though passion may have strained, it must not break our bonds of affection. The mystic chords of memory will swell when again touched, as surely they will be, by the better angels of our nature."

The Fragile Truth

August 27, 2020

"Look around, look around! How lucky we are to be alive right now!"

That line is from the musical "Hamilton." The Schuyler sisters live in New York City at the dawn of the American Revolution. While they acknowledge the danger of imminent war, they sing their excitement in soaring harmonies.

But as deaths from COVID-19 climb toward 200,000 in our country, I hear the same words as a lament. Look around, look around. How lucky we are to be alive ... at all.

This grim reality barely registered a blip during the Republican National Convention. There was a noticeable lack of facemasks and social distancing among the crowds. Few speakers made mention of the pandemic, their heads in the proverbial sand.

The first lady was a notable exception.

Melania Trump expressed sympathy for mourners and praised the men and women who help "when we are at our most fragile." This "fragile" admission stood out in a convention that styled itself a crusade for law and order.

Strength is the goal of a political convention. Whether referring to bones, egos or presidents, "fragile" hardly has a positive connotation. The Latin root of fragile means, not surprisingly, "easily broken." If something is fragile, then it must be handled with care. By the 16th century, the term was spiritualized as "morally weak" and "liable to sin." And by 1858, there was the first documented reference to a "fragile" person as someone who was physically sick.

It seems that Republicans do not believe that identifying with such fragility will win votes. Yet, psychologist Susan David has proven that strength comes from acknowledging our fragility.

David lost her father to cancer when she was only 15 years old. Back then, if someone asked how she was doing, she would reply, "OK." She was praised for being strong and independent. She might have gone onto a career as a politician …

But David's eighth-grade English teacher didn't buy this facade.

This teacher handed her a blank notebook with the instructions to "write like nobody's reading." This freed the grieving teenager to express her true feelings, and David now claims this honesty made all the difference both in terms of her emotional well-being and future career. As a psychologist, she has dedicated her life's work to helping others.

The truth sets us free (John 8:32).

I say to all of us: Look around, look around! Things are not "OK." Melania Trump spoke of "the invisible enemy COVID-19." Not only is the virus invisible, but many of the dying are unseen. They are in nursing homes, low-income neighborhoods and prisons. The majority of the dead are either elderly, immigrants or people of color — people who are often overlooked even in healthy times. The "lucky" or privileged among us can choose to ignore the suffering.

If we would look beyond ourselves, then the truth can set us free to serve others with compassion. In this fragile time, more of us can look to help the most vulnerable or "least among us" (Matthew 25) instead of putting up a political facade — the lie that our current response to the coronavirus has been "great."

A Conspiracy Theory with Wings

September 3, 2020

We have not one but two "Plandemic" conspiracy theory films, both of which falsely assert that the coronavirus was "planned" by powerful people in order to make their fortune. Even though Judy Mikovits, a former research scientist, has been discredited and her claims about the coronavirus proven to be misleading or outright lies, a second video has surfaced to spread more false information.

A conspiracy theory often cherry-picks facts, then assembles them to create the appearance of an argument. But just because I picked a bird feather from the ground, a battery from a smoke detector and a chair from my kitchen table doesn't mean that I've made a machine that will fly.

Neither should these "Plandemic" theories have ever gotten off the ground, much less become viral videos.

While conspiracy theories have existed for decades — such as the claim that the landing on the moon was fake — we now find these otherworldly claims are given the light of national attention rather than tucked away in the dark corners of the political fringe.

The president of the United States frequently tweets the conspiracy theories of a group known as QAnon, which claims — without evidence, mind you — that President Trump is battling a "deep state" primarily composed of Hollywood elites who wish to destroy America.

I received a mailing attacking Cal Cunningham, the Democratic candidate for the Senate, as "Communist Cal." I looked to see what special interest right-wing group paid for this propaganda, but I was dismayed that it was the Republican Party of North Carolina. Not a word about policy in a time of a global pandemic and economic recession. Their political platform is a conspiracy theory.

Modern conspiracy theories result in division. Instead of the common good, the goal is to pit people against one another. To yell accusations at one another and point fingers of blame. Political, civil and religious leaders fan these flames in order to stay in power rather than work with others to solve problems.

Yet, the word conspiracy is derived from the Latin "con-spiritus" which did not refer to paranoia, fantasy or falsehoods. It meant "to breathe together."

Long ago, there was a brown-skinned homeless man who wandered the Galilean countryside bringing people together. This fellow knew full well the power of the Roman Empire, yet he plotted and planned to overcome the might of the sword with the power of forgiveness, hope and most of all love. He breathed on his followers, then sent them into the world to be peacemakers (John 20:21–22).

Maybe such a holy conspiracy will take wings and soar.

Peace Train Take This Country
September 10, 2020

"Now I've been crying lately, thinking about the world as it is. Why must we go on hating?"

Those lyrics are from the song "Peace Train" written by Cat Stevens in 1971, but the verses make me think of the year 2001, specifically 9/11. I was an undergraduate student at a small liberal arts college in western North Carolina. When America invaded Iraq, I participated in peace rallies. I used to hold a handmade sign that read, "Jesus said Love Your Enemies, not Drop Bombs on Them."

Not everyone appreciated this message. This was the time of "freedom fries," the fast-food staple renamed by one of the Tar Heel State's members of Congress because of France's opposition to the war. Never mind that french fries don't actually come from France.

My fellow protesters and I played "Peace Train" at those rallies, but the songwriter was in the national headlines for different reasons. He had changed his name to Yusuf Islam after he became a Muslim. He found out that he was on America's "no fly" list after he was pulled from a plane by FBI agents.

There has never been a credible link that connects Yusaf Islam to terrorists. In fact, he had been vocal in condemning the 9/11 attacks, maintaining it was "absolutely imperative that people get to know the real Islam. ... When something is wrong, it's wrong, you know; it's totally abhorrent, and we totally condemn (the attacks on 9/11)."

The word "Islam" is from the Arabic for "peace" — salaam. The Quran states: "Make peace between your brothers and be conscious of God so that hopefully you will gain mercy." This is the spirit of the real Islam as practiced by 1.5 billion believers across the globe.

Fundamentalists, whether Muslim or Christian, highjack a few verses of sacred scripture and ignore the essential values of the faith tradition. This was true of the terrorists responsible for 9/11. It remains true of today's politicians and other public figures who interpret the actions of a few Muslims as indicative of the entire religion. As a result, hate crimes have increased, and Islamophobia is once again on the rise in our country. When something is wrong, it's wrong and should be named — things like terrorism, racial stereotyping and religious discrimination.

When something is right, it's right. Jesus did say, "Love your enemies," and also, "Blessed are the peacemakers." He added that we would recognize peacemakers by "their fruits." We know if people bear the fruit of peace by what they say and do.

Since the coronavirus pandemic, my church has adopted a "watchword" — a verse of scripture meant to guide us through a difficult time. I share John 14:27 with you, gentle reader, in hopes it will inspire you whether you share my religion or not:

"Peace I leave to you. My peace I give to you. I do not give as the world gives. Do not let your hearts be troubled, and do not be afraid."

Though fundamentalists pervert such a message of peace and some politicians fan the flames of fear, everyone of good faith can build bridges, using scripture and tradition to seek the common ground that unites us all. Together, we can realize the dream of salaam. It gives me hope as I sing these "Peace Train" lyrics:

"I've been smiling lately, dreaming about the world as one. ... Peace train take this country, come take me home again."

The Signs of the Apocalypse

September 17, 2020

The late writer David Foster Wallace began a 2005 commencement speech with this parable: There were two young fish swimming along, and they happened to meet an older fish swimming the other way who nodded at them and said, "Morning, boys. How's the water?" The two young fish continued, and then eventually one of them looked over at the other and said, "What the hell is water?"

As Wallace stated, this little story makes the large point that "the most obvious, important realities are often the ones that are hardest to see and talk about."

Apocalyptic literature is written to allow us to see and talk about these obvious, important realities.

"Apocalypse" does not mean the end of time. It does not necessarily imply catastrophe or doom. Apocalypse means to reveal — to reveal what has been right in front of us, what we've been swimming in the whole time. It's graphic in order to get our attention.

Many religions have such attention-grabbing scriptures. In the New Testament, the Book of Revelation is infamous for its predictions of a bloody future. But the opening chapters consist of letters to seven different churches that reveal what those churches are to do in the present.

In our time, we have seen terrifying, tragic images of burning forests, smokey skies and survivors picking through charred houses.

Yet do we see the obvious connection to climate change?

People continue to deny the hotter temperatures and the drier forests are results of global warming. It's not that the scientific evidence is complicated. Certain politicians don't want to acknowledge the truth right in front of their faces, even as the country burns. By and large, our society doesn't want to change our economy's reliance upon fossil fuels that produce carbon emissions.

Individuals can take steps to reduce their carbon footprint. We are also responsible for holding our elected officials accountable for real and lasting plans to reduce carbon emissions and to curb climate change.

Before it is too late.

I realize that some dispute the "truth" of climate change. In his commencement address, Wallace spoke of the capital-T Truth. Not political spin. Neither public opinion nor religious dogma. Climate change is the capital-T Truth of life BEFORE death. Unless our political leaders commit to drastically reducing heat-trapping pollution that is warming our world, temperatures will continue to rise, resulting in more fires, greater destruction and increased loss of life.

It is also true that the most important realities are often the ones that are hardest to see and talk about. It seems to me that science alone will not persuade enough of us, quickly enough, to change our course. But perhaps the orange skies and smoke-filled air are revelations about a deadly future. Perhaps these apocalyptic images will inspire the change that statistics cannot do alone. That is why the ancients wrote texts full of graphic images — they knew that behaviors would change if hearts and minds are changed first.

Thinking again of those young fish in the parable, our question is no longer, "What the hell is going on?" The science of climate change is clear. This apocalyptic moment reveals a more urgent, personal question:

What the heck are we going to do about it?

A Case for Charity: RBG

September 24, 2020

"And now abideth faith, hope, charity, these three; but the greatest of these is charity."

This New Testament text is likely familiar because it is often read at weddings, whether the ceremony is Christian or not. Likely familiar, that is, except for one word: "Charity" is usually translated as "love."

Charity is a word that may cause many to stumble, for the term calls to mind an action or event that helps a specific person or community in need. But, as used in the New Testament, this particular kind of love — agape — is not just about a tax write-off.

It is love, but neither the stuff of a Hallmark card nor any warm fuzzy.

This idea of charity/love is one of action. It is to do justice — to do all one can to ensure that the standards, practices and laws are applied fairly and equitably to all.

It makes me think of the recently deceased associate justice of the Supreme Court, Ruth Bader Ginsberg,

Before she became a judge, the Notorious RBG (as she later came to be known) successfully argued five cases before the Supreme Court that have had wide-ranging consequences for women ever since. The genius of this young lawyer was to fight the imbalance of power in favor of men by arguing for gender equality on behalf of *male* plaintiffs.

My favorite example is the case of Weinberger v. Wiesenfeld. In 1972, Stephen Wiesenfeld's wife, Paula Wiesenfeld, died in childbirth. According to the law at that time, this widower was not entitled to his wife's Social Security benefits, even though he was struggling to raise their child on his own. The assumption of the law was that a man was the primary wage earner in a household, which was not true in the Wiesenfelds' marriage.

Thinking this was unfair, Stephen Wiesenfeld wrote a letter to the editor of the local newspaper — and the rest is history.

Ginsburg argued before the highest court that the Social Security Act of 1935 discriminated against men like Wiesenfeld based solely on their gender. Before an all-male Supreme Court, she won a unanimous verdict and simultaneously legitimized women's payments into the Social Security system.

Here's the icing on the cake — the wedding cake! Forty years after the verdict, Ginsburg officiated Wiesenfeld's second marriage.

The case of Weinberger v. Wiesenfeld demonstrates that a hallmark of justice is that the same rationale is applied to different decisions. Without waiting for the results of a president election in less than six weeks, Senator Mitch McConnell, Republican and Senate majority leader, vowed to hold a vote on President Donald Trump's nominee to the Supreme Court to replace RBG.

In 2016, this same senator prevented President Barack Obama's nominee to the Supreme Court from reaching the Senate floor for 10 *months*, claiming, "The American people are perfectly capable of having their say on this issue, so let's give them a voice. Let's let the American people decide. The Senate will appropriately revisit the matter when it considers the qualifications of the nominee the next president nominates, whoever that might be."

Now that a member of *his* party is the president, McConnell clearly wants to have his cake and eat it too.

I say to McConnell, be charitable in the sense of consistency and fairness.

Still, even if justice is not served in this particular case, RBG gives me hope: "So often in life, things that you regard as an impediment turn out to be great, good fortune."

Prayers for President Trump

October 1, 2020

I pray for Donald J. Trump.

I am dismayed by his administration's mismanagement of the COVID-19 crisis. By his own admission to reporter Bob Woodward, Trump has downplayed the severity of this deadly disease. He continues to contradict and dismiss the scientific and medical opinion of experts, as well as his own advisers, which has had the effect of distorting the truth and dividing Americans.

Just a week before he was infected, Trump told a rally of supporters that the disease "affects virtually nobody." He made this claim as the deaths in this country alone topped 200,000 people.

The president has played politics with the public health.

Now that Trump has tested positive for COVID-19, I pray for his speedy recovery, for to celebrate in the suffering of others is wicked.

But what will be the lingering effects of this president's COVID-19 on the national response to the pandemic?

It is true that this virus affects people differently. Even certain people with the same high-risk factors as Trump (age and obesity) recover fairly quickly.

Would his speedy recovery not fuel this president's falsehoods that the virus is essentially harmless? Would this not embolden his supporters, as well as a percentage of the larger public, to flaunt the best practices of precaution and safety?

As I pray for the president to recover, I also pray for a change in his attitude.

Perhaps this prayer seems futile. This president has shown little regard for those who think differently than him. He has demonstrated little remorse for his mistakes, let alone displayed the humility necessary to accept responsibility for his errors.

He could have a change of heart.

Witness the story of the exodus in the Hebrew Bible. After Moses parted the Red Sea so the Israelites could flee to the other side, the waters closed over the pursuing Egyptian Army. In the words of the African American spiritual, "Pharaoh's Army done got drown!" From the safety of the far shoreline, the Israelites celebrated the defeat of the Egyptians with dance and song (see Exodus, chapter 15).

But later rabbinical tradition taught a much different lesson by imagining the scene in heaven. When the angels celebrated the deaths of Israel's opponents, God rebuked them: "Are these drowned Egyptians not also my children?"

To celebrate the suffering of others is wicked. The best lights of many religions and philosophies teach compassion and care toward all people.

May Trump imagine the pain and grief of the hundreds of thousands who have suffered and grieved in this country. May he listen to the overwhelming scientific opinion about the best ways to prevent infection and set a good example by wearing a mask in public and maintaining social distance. May he require his supporters to do the same at his campaign rallies.

Instead of playing politics with public health as a means of seeking reelection, may President Trump rally everyone in this country to prevent the spread of this deadly disease.

In praying this prayer for our president, may you and I model such grace as well.

Hollering Before the Election

October 8, 2020

Recently, my wife vacationed at the beach for three nights with her parents. It was a well-deserved and much need respite for her.

Our three children spent a night with me in our home, then all of us decamped to my parents' house in Raleigh. After topping off a lovely visit with Nana's pumpkin pancakes, the kids and I returned to our place ahead of their mother. I had designs on getting the house in order before she arrived.

But as I unloaded the minivan, our 5-year-old son ran out of the house.

"Daddy, there's an emergency in your bedroom!"

I dropped the suitcases and took the steps three at a time. I saw the puddle on the carpet first. Then the baseball-sized bulge in the ceiling, dripping water.

I rushed up to the third floor and shut off the valves to the bathroom sink and toilet. I raced back downstairs. If anything, the drip was faster, and the bulge was bigger. Back up the stairs to the attic where I began hauling out boxes of photo albums, Christmas decorations and battery-operated toys that play music.

Our three children watched quietly until those toys hit the light of their playroom. Then, kids and toys sprang to life noisily, but for once I was too distracted to care about umpteen repeats of Old MacDonald.

Finally, I cleared a path to the water heater and saw the soaked plywood.

My readers should know that I have little knowledge about any home appliance. I've rented for the vast majority of my adult life. If something didn't work, I called the landlord.

Now that I pay a bank for the privilege of living in a home, the buck stops here.

I did the only thing I knew how to do. I ran all the way downstairs into the backyard and hollered for my neighbor.

As usual, he was in the midst of his own home repair project. We first bonded over friendly discussions while he was rebuilding his front porch. Last fall, he installed a replacement garbage disposal for me for the price of beers. This summer, we have shared a few more frosty beverages.

But when I called for him, he immediately halted his project and rushed around our fence. He helped me shut off the water heater and mop up while I began the project of drying the bedroom carpet.

A water leak can be a disaster. But thanks to a little luck and a helping hand, this particular leak is going to be fine. It cost me 30 minutes of stress as well as a few cold showers. But I imagine that, by the time you read these words, I'll have a new water heater.

According to the latest polls, you and I will also have a new president in less than a month. Based on our previous conversations, I don't think that my neighbor would like that change. But I know that he offered to help fix the drywall on my ceiling. He tells me to holler if I need anything at all.

That gives me hope not only for my home but for our country.

The Most Important Choices Are Ours to Make

October 15, 2020

The last question of this year's vice-presidential debate was posed by a middle schooler named Brecklynn Brown: "If our leaders can't get along, how are the citizens supposed to get along?"

Each candidate praised this question, and, in turn, I thought there was merit in both their responses. Vice President Mike Pence pointed to the model of friendship between conservative Supreme Court Justice Antonin Scalia and liberal Justice Ruth Bader Ginsberg. Sen. Kamala Harris emphasized that Brown and her peers can make a difference despite partisan rancor.

For me, Brecklynn Brown's question brought a Cherokee legend to mind. A child confesses to her grandmother that she feels a terrible battle in her heart and mind between two wolves — the struggle between the positive force of kindness, hope and compassion versus the negative force of anger, greed and arrogance. The child wants to know which wolf will win.

The grandmother responds, "The one you choose to feed will win."

It's no myth that there are real struggles in America today. Communities, such as ours in Chatham County, are torn by economic, racial and gender inequalities. The gaps between the haves and the have-nots are not mere talking points on a debate stage but make the difference between life and death. It is estimated that one in five Americans suffers food insecurity. People are literally starving in the richest country in the world.

The hope, however, is that, if we recognize the severity of these problems, then we can choose to be part of the solutions. We can choose to feed the generous, gracious parts of ourselves in order to help those in need. This choice will cause us to find common ground despite political differences. And we the people can lead the way by setting the example for our leaders.

The writer Wendell Berry draws a distinction between Big Thought and Think Little. Big Thought is the work of an organization or institution like the federal government. Think Little, Berry explains, represents an individual "who is trying to live as a neighbor to their neighbors." That person "will have a lively and practical understanding of the work of peace and brotherhood and let there be no mistake about it — that person is doing that work."

That person can be Brecklynn Brown, you and me. I would say that work is our sacred responsibility.

In her editorial for the New York Times, novelist Marilynne Robinson wrote, "If someone is hungry, feed him. He will be thirsty, so be sure that he has good water to drink. If he is in prison, don't abuse, abandon or exploit him, or assume that he ought to be there. If these problems afflict whole populations, those with influence or authority should repent and do better, as all the prophets tell them." Using Berry's distinction, Big Thought and Think Little should work together in order to help the least of those among us.

Robinson's editorial reminds me of a parable in the Gospel of Matthew that involves the struggle for the soul of the nation. Every country in the world comes before the judgment throne, yet the nations are not sorted based on political or religious distinctions. According to the parable, there is a most important question: What did you do for the least of those among you — the hungry, the poor, the incarcerated?

Robinson challenges all of us, saying, "We are asked to see one another in the light of a singular inalienable worth that would make a family of us if we let it."

The choice is ours.

Dreams of Dog Days

October 22, 2020

Give me this one fantasy.

I want a dog.

I grew up with a half-Lab, half-Golden Retriever named Lucy. Right out of college, I adopted a puppy I named after the poet Nikki Giovanni. Before she died, Nikki lived with me across two states as I married and had two sons. Now my wife and I have a third child, a daughter, and our young family is crammed into a 1,700 square-foot home with a backyard I can spit across. And I want a dog.

Our youngest is my accomplice. She wants to take home every canine she encounters in the neighborhood. Her two older brothers are skittish around dogs, which to my mind is another reason to get one. The middle child was bit when he was about his sister's age. He needs a new, positive experience.

I need a new, positive experience.

More than seven months have passed since the first case of the coronavirus in North Carolina. This past Friday set a record high in new infections. For me, a dog represents a return to normalcy. A simpler time when the flu was the only vaccine I thought about on a regular basis. In her poem "Small Kindnesses," Danusha Laméris reminds us that saying, "bless you" after a sneeze is "a leftover / from the Bubonic plague." We had turned a deadly fear into a polite response. Now a sneeze is no longer just a sneeze.

Such is my desire for an idealized, simpler past that I even started a dinner conversation about the perfect name for our fictional dog. Our daughter's suggestions — Flower and Clover — elicited groans from her brothers. The boys like the names Force and Fire, both of which are non-starters with their parents. Finally, their mother suggested Moon. I envisioned a white-haired puppy, a Husky mix with blue eyes. Perfect.

The very next weekend my daughter and I encountered a black Lab on a neighborhood walk. The dog's name was Luna. A sign from the heavens!

Though willing to humor me, my wife is quick to point out that we don't have the space in our home for another life force, much less the time or energy. We are already stretched too thin between pastoring two churches and our eldest's virtual classroom. In the parlance of our time, we don't have enough bandwidth. I'm tired of that metaphor, for I'm tired of the computer. Tired of Zoom calls and emails. I'm so tired of being tired.

I woke up early to scratch these thoughts on the back of my daughter's discarded painting. My days run together like her watercolors.

But I remember carefree days with my dog Nikki. When she was a puppy, I'd walk her to the park near my crummy, one-bedroom apartment and she'd try to eat goose poop. Ah, those were good ole days! A few years later, my wife and I walked Nikki down the city streets of Richmond. Then came after-dinner walks with one of us holding the leash, the other pushing the stroller.

The holidays are coming. I daydream about our kids running downstairs on Christmas morning and can almost hear squeals of delight over the white-haired puppy in my arms. As our kids fawn over her soft fur and pale blue eyes, Moon gently licks their faces. My wife lovingly catches my eye. I would never say I told you so.

I'm under no illusion that we will magically return to a time when a sneeze is just a sneeze. But give me this one fantasy.

A Poll Chaplain on Election Day
November 5, 2020

I was contacted a few weeks ago to serve as a volunteer "poll chaplain" — a nonpartisan, unanxious presence on Election Day. The nonprofit that made the request hoped that chaplains would deter hostile acts and possibly even de-escalate dangerous incidents of voter intimidation.

The polls opened at 6:30 that morning, but I was awake even earlier. I'll admit I was a little nervous. Staring out the window, I reflected on the bright moon shining over all of us: Democrats, Republicans and everyone else in our hemisphere. As the moon faded, what would this day reveal?

The day was bright and sunny. I wore a clerical collar for the first time in my life as part of my poll chaplain uniform. Over the course of the day, no one addressed me as Father, which was too bad because I had prepared a cheesy comeback — "Actually, my kids call me *Dad*."

I also donned a white facemask to match my new clerical collar. Volunteers from the two major political parties had gathered under separate tents. Each camp had pamphlets and flyers to hand out to voters. But only one group wore face masks.

I lament that public health has become a partisan issue.

I knew that my county had the highest percentage of mailed ballots in the state. Even so, I was not prepared for the slow trickle of voters throughout the day.

The volunteers and I did what you do when you find yourself waiting under a gorgeous Carolina blue sky. We made small talk. Someone's son attended my alma mater. I'd visited someone else's home church in Pittsburgh. I met a gentleman who had attended my father's church last Christmas Eve.

Our conversation steered clear of politics. But we did talk religion, including the Heart Sutra — one of the most popular Buddhist meditation chants. I could recite the first few words from memory which pleased that particular volunteer.

With others, I spoke of the religions of baseball and fishing. An elderly woman told me about her "lucky spot" for fishing in the local river. I asked if I could try it out with my kids. She smiled, "There's plenty of fish to go around."

I saw no signs of voter intimidation. There was nothing hostile or troublesome. At the end of the day, I posed at a social distance for pictures with volunteers from both tents.

Back home, I helped get the kids in bed. Before tuning in to the election results, I once again looked up at the Man in the Moon. I thought about how the real human faces are much closer, but I don't always take the time to observe them, much less learn about their favorite fishing holes.

I doubt I'll make a habit of wearing a clerical collar — it's too tight around my neck! But from my experience as a poll chaplain, I'll remember the holy moments I caught in the human moments — a smile, a story, a connection. Despite the things that divide us, what if there really is plenty of kindness to go around? As the Heart Sutra ends, svaha: "So be it."

Woody Guthrie and the Magic Word

November 12, 2020

Woody Guthrie's song "This Land Is Your Land" is recognizable to millions by the chorus:

"This land was made for you and me."

This folk classic celebrates the gift of America. The verses are filled with the beauty of the country and a love for its best ideals. The song also insists on inclusion — you *and* me. "And" is the magic word.

Our country has had two political parties from its inception, and citizens have been bitterly divided in the past. This is especially true today after our most recent presidential election. The election map shows the geographical splits. Blue America and Red America are further divided over cultural, racial and socio-economic differences.

We settle for you *or* me.

For many of us, the challenge is more than the fact that we do not understand the other side. We do not wish to learn about those folks because we do not trust them.

Therefore, we need a focus that can unite us — help us to see our country as both/and, not either/or. Guthrie offered such words.

Guthrie was born in Oklahoma in the early part of the 20th century. He experienced firsthand the poverty of the Dust Bowl era as well as the Great Depression. As a child, he also suffered the personal tragedies of the loss of his home in a fire and the death of his mother.

These experiences shaped Guthrie's vision of America as much as the natural beauty of the environment. He identified with people who were hungry, poor and downtrodden. While "This Land Is Your Land" is best known by its chorus, a verse includes these lines: "In the shadow of the steeple I saw my people, by the relief office I seen my people."

Notice how Guthrie stressed that the people in need were "my people." He not only cared for them, but he also identified with them. This calls to mind another man who roamed and rambled even longer ago:

"Truly I tell you, just as you did it to one of the least of those among you, you did it to me."

Matthew 25:40 is one of the more famous teachings of Jesus. Yet, the mandate to care for those in need is by no means limited to Christianity. At a time when millions of Americans suffer from the great recession caused by the coronavirus, the need is now. Service to others could unite us across our religious differences as well as our politics. People of good faith could reach out in kindness, care and what the New Testament terms "brotherly love" (philos).

My 5-year-old son thinks his big brother hung the moon and stars. He wants to do everything like his hero. Recently, his big brother decided to teach him how to read. The first lesson involved a certain conjunction. I heard them reading together on the couch, the older one pausing when he reached that magic word in the text so that the younger could chime in: "And … and … and …"

That one word can make magic.

Vaccines and Our Holy Cause

November 19, 2020

After my recent eye exam, the receptionist informed me that she would not get the flu vaccine because she has gotten the flu as a result. I have heard this argument before.

In his timely guest editorial in the Chatham News + Record, Dr. John Dykers warned against this very mistaken assumption. The problem is that people typically wait too long to get the shot and then catch the flu before the vaccine has taken effect in their immune systems. According to Dr. Dykers, "Then you would tell others the shot caused flu when it did not."

People mistake correlation with causation. My last three optometrists have all been Roman Catholic, but I don't jump to conclusions and claim that all optometrists must be Catholic or argue that all Catholics raise their children to become optometrists!

There is a false yet persistent claim that certain vaccines cause cognitive impairment in children. While I'm sure there are kids with autism who have been vaccinated, the medical community has proven that vaccines do not produce neurodevelopmental disorders. Causation and correlation are not the same thing.

Last week, we learned about a new COVID-19 vaccine from Pfizer. Dr. Anthony Fauci called the results "extraordinary." Yet, even if the new coronavirus vaccine proves to be as effective among the general population as in Pfizer's clinical trials, surveys have shown that a significant percentage of the American public will not be vaccinated.

In terms of my eye doctors, I do not want them to decide my lens prescription based on blind faith. I want to look at the data. Americans should think the same about vaccines.

Let's be clear: In order for the most vulnerable and at-risk members of a population to be protected from an infectious disease, the rest of us must be vaccinated. The American public needs to be on the same page. Yet, myths about vaccinations persist. And people do not comply.

Like Dr. Dykers, I want to convince so-called "anti-vaxxers" that the proof of vaccinations is in the science — not in anecdotal evidence or limited personal experience. To the chorus of physicians and public health officials, I add my voice as a theologian.

The wisdom and genius of many religions and worldviews is that, by envisioning a Higher Power who so loves the world, we are motivated to care for the welfare of our fellow creatures. Because we understand that each life is part of the fabric of creation, we make ethical judgments not merely about what is advantageous for an individual or small group but what is most life-giving for the common good. That is a holy cause.

Causation and correlation are not the same thing. This mistake is often ridiculous. For instance, I've known exactly three white guys named Marcus and all of them have been Lutheran pastors. Let's not jump to conclusions ...

And let's not make deadly misunderstandings about vaccines.

A Giving of Thanks

November 26, 2020

The past year has wrought a global pandemic, a heated election, scores of wildfires and the worst hurricane season ever recorded — and the hits keep coming. The third wave of the coronavirus looms over winter. A much-needed economic stimulus remains in jeopardy. Intractable leaders dig in their heels.

Still, as in years past, we have set aside the fourth Thursday in November to give thanks.

Thanksgiving began in 1863. Not exactly a peaceful and prosperous year. To quote the president of the time, our nation was "in the midst of a civil war of unequalled magnitude and severity." The same Abraham Lincoln issued the Thanksgiving proclamation, declaring a national holiday so that "gracious gifts ... should be solemnly, reverently and gratefully acknowledged as with one heart and voice by the whole American people."

I appreciate the call to gratitude as well as the appeal for unity. But gratitude is not another thing I "should" do. "Should" is a strict taskmaster, a joyless disciplinarian. We command our small children to say thank you, forgetting that a true giving of thanks is neither compelled nor coerced.

Gratitude comes unbidden like a sudden breeze, the family dog, a child's laughter.

When my younger brother turned 3, maybe 4 years old, our grandmother presented him with a gift bag. White tissue paper billowed from the top. The little boy grinned, "You gave me tissue paper to blow my nose! Thank you!" He was happy with the present he eventually unwrapped, but while the toy has been forgotten, our family has remembered his gratitude for the wrapping paper.

If the year 2020 were to present a gift, I would expect the bag to be empty and 2020 to cackle, "Gotcha again!"

But genuine gratitude is never empty of grace.

I sit by the window most mornings and watch for the first fingers of dawn. Gradually, the pine trees come into view as dark exclamation points against the fiery sky. Those rascal squirrels begin their usual mischief. Chickadees run their mad errands. A mourning dove coos and hoots like the tuning of a lonely woodwind instrument.

Soon enough, I will get to work on all the things I "should" do.

First, I give thanks for the trees, the birds, the squirrels. The slanting morning light through the rising steam of my coffee. Oatmeal bubbling on the stove. My wife and children upstairs, tucked under their warm covers.

Great leaders, like Lincoln, may tell us what we should do. But a child squeals at the tissue paper — the simple detail we might have ignored or tossed aside. And that would be our loss.

A giving of thanks is itself a gift.

A Simple, Sublime Light

December 3, 2020

George Harrison was known as the quiet Beatle. He was not as famous as John Lennon, Paul McCartney or Ringo Starr. Yet, he is my favorite member of the band. He was a gardener, a spiritual singer and the writer of my favorite Beatles' song "Here Comes the Sun."

The song has only a couple of chords. A very mediocre guitar player like I am can more or less hack the tune. The lyrics are repetitive and simple. The studio recording is only three minutes long. The song is simple — simply sublime.

Harrison picks out each note in perfect syncopation with his soft vocals. "Here Comes the Sun" is the most downloaded Beatles song of all time. It is a masterpiece.

Though written in 1969, the lyrics are particularly poignant in this time of the coronavirus. The past year has felt like "a long, cold, lonely winter." But lately I have seen "the smiles returning to the faces." Not just one but several vaccines are on the horizon. The future promises brighter days. Hope rises like the sun.

The metaphor of hope as the rising sun is likewise found in simple, sublime scriptures. Weeping may linger for the night, but joy shall come in the morning (Psalm 30:5). People who have walked in darkness have seen a great light (Isaiah 9:2). Morning by morning, new mercies I see (Lamentations 3:23).

For Christians, the season of Advent has dawned. This is the time when we look for the coming of the Son — the Son of God who is the light that shines in the darkness (John 1:5).

Many other religions evoke metaphors of light, specifically the sunrise as a symbol of rebirth and new life. Harrison became a devotee of Eastern spirituality. He studied the ancient Hindu text, the Bhagavad Gita, in which the god Krishna appeared to a warrior named Arjuna during a great battle. Harrison interpreted the text as an allegory for the spiritual struggle to find hope in the chaos of life.

I've heard "Here Comes the Sun" my whole life in places as diverse as skating rinks and baseball parks, in movie theaters and elevators, during weddings and funerals. This uplifting song can give hope even at the graveside. Harrison died at the age of 58 years because of a respiratory illness (lung cancer). In addition to his music, he left us with these bright words:

"Look for the light. The light is within you."

Vaccines are on the horizon, yet we must be cautious into the foreseeable future. COVID-19 is still a threat. Infections are rising along with hospitalizations and the death toll.

While we wait for a new time, we can listen to the quiet Beatle. I encourage us to use this time of relative solitude and isolation to contemplate the simple, sublime truths. For illumination, we can sing of bright hope — "Here comes the sun, do-do-do."

Christmas with the Beatles

December 10, 2020

Since the church I pastor cannot gather to sing Christmas carols due to the threat of spreading COVID-19, I've had a different soundtrack this year. No silent nights or decking the halls. There have been "merry gentlemen," but their names are Paul, George and John. And a little drummer boy named Ringo.

The Beatles did not record a Christmas record, but songs like "All You Need Is Love" and "With a Little Help from My Friends" are meaningful this time of year and poignant during this pandemic.

I have also found inspiration from the life stories of these musicians. COVID-19 has made it clear that there are forces beyond our control. Famous or not, tragedy happens. How will we respond?

Long before he was knighted by Queen Elizabeth II, Sir Paul McCartney was a skinny teenager who lost his mother to breast cancer. He was only 14 years old when she died.

McCartney happened to meet another youth in Liverpool, England, whose mother had also died young. That youth's name was John Lennon. These two teenagers played guitar together. They took another kid under their wing. George Harrison became like a little brother.

Flash forward 10 years. The Beatles had become the most recognizable rock band in the world. McCartney had more fortune and fame than he could have imagined growing up as the son of working-class parents.

Yet, he was miserable.

He feuded with Lennon. He tried to play peacemaker, but the band was on the verge of breaking up. By his own admission, McCartney coped by using drugs and alcohol.

Then he had a dream.

His mother, Mary, appeared to him and told him that everything was going to be all right. McCartney woke up with a feeling of peace and also a melody in his head.

"I wake up to the sound of music, Mother Mary comes to me, speaking words of wisdom, let it be."

Though "Let It Be" is played around the world, is it the best advice? We hear messages like "Tough It Out" or "Figure It Out." Such advice may be useful in certain times.

But around Christmas, another mother Mary comes to mind.

Long before the Beatles, this young woman was told she would bear the son of the Most High God. And this Mary, being a virgin, responded, "How can it be?"

The angel Gabriel assured her, "Nothing will be impossible with God."

Mary replied, "Let it be."

I read this story in the Gospel of Luke. A friend in Pittsburgh texted that, while pushing her infant son in the stroller, she had seen trucks carrying the coronavirus vaccine driving toward the main hospital. My friend broke down in tears thinking about how, perhaps even sooner than she had hoped, she would be able to hug her friends again. That day will feel like Christmas.

Until then, stay safe. Wear masks. Keep your distance. Use Zoom video conferences or Google Hangout. No, it's not the same.

But let it be.

As you wait, pull out your Beatles' albums or cue the music on your computer. Pull out an old acoustic guitar and try to pick out the melody. Sing the faith.

"And when the night is cloudy, there is still a light that shines on me. Shine on until tomorrow, let it be."

Dear Santa: Can We Talk about the Postal Service?

December 17, 2020

Dear Santa,

How are you? I don't know about the rate of COVID-19 infections in the North Pole, but they are steadily increasing here. You probably already knew that — you check your list twice.

I'm curious if, during the pandemic, more of your business has shifted to virtual platforms. Has fiber optic internet cable made it out to Santa's workshop?

Please don't think I'm shouting or pouting. There are many advantages to technology.

But I'm grateful to write an old-fashioned letter to you. It reminds me of the simpler times when I was a kid. I also receive so many emails that a three-dimensional envelope in the mailbox seems like a godsend.

The way things are going, it might soon be a miracle.

Santa, our postal system is in trouble. The other day, our church received a number of envelopes that had been postmarked Nov. 12. I don't need to remind you how many days there are until Christmas!

Please don't misunderstand me: I'm not suggesting that the men and women in the local and regional post offices — the mail processors, handlers and carriers — should be on your Naughty List. In fact, the mailwoman for my neighborhood delivers every piece of mail with a smile.

The problem is that certain government officials had a vested interest in slowing down the mail delivery system before our recent national election. Louis DeJoy, the new postmaster general, has cut the budget, laid off employees and put a blanket ban on overtime for Postal Service workers. This Grinch has even instructed mail carriers to leave packages behind if doing so can speed up their routes.

For goodness sake, Santa! Imagine instructing your elves to forget a few children's gifts in the name of efficiency!

Not everyone uses a digital highway, much less a sleigh pulled by flying reindeer. We need our postal service, especially this year when many of us will not see our loved ones in person.

I want you to know that my 5-year-old son has put his letter to you in the mail. His big brother helped him write it. The younger one drew the pictures.

My younger son also mailed another card. I have an aunt who lives several hours away. During COVID, the distance has seemed even farther because we cannot safely visit. She is a widow, and the holidays were hard enough. This year, she will be alone.

My son decorated her Christmas card all by himself. He drew a self-portrait with his arms spread wide in a hug. He also colored a picture of our house, running outside to double-check the number of windows for accuracy. He wanted his great aunt to remember exactly what our house looked like because someday she will visit again.

Finally, the pièce de resistance, he drew a bright green poop emoji — "Just to make her smile, Dad."

Santa, I think those Scrooges in the federal government deserve lumps of coal in their stockings this year. But that's your decision.

My Christmas wish is that my fellow citizens will support our postal workers. You of all people know that, while packages come in different shapes and sizes, the greatest gift is love.

Thanks for your timely deliveries, Santa. We'll leave cookies for you by the tree — the real thing! No emojis.

Sincerely yours,

Andrew

Don't Be a Goldfish

January 7, 2021

Over the Christmas holiday, my wife and I watched all 10 episodes of "Ted Lasso." Actor Jason Sudeikis plays the title character — a moustache-wearing former coach of a small-college football team who is hired to lead a premier soccer team in England. Of course, in Great Britain (along with the rest of the world), soccer is called "football" and this television show features hilarious cross-cultural lessons, many at the expense of the American coach.

But coach Lasso gamely shares his own eccentric twists on time-honored wisdom. He tells a struggling player that the happiest animal is the goldfish because this creature has a 10-second memory. Be a goldfish, Lasso advises.

I played baseball growing up and often heard a similar idea. I'd make a mistake and the coach would yell, "Forget about it!" You couldn't dwell on an error or strikeout because it would hinder you from doing your best the next time a ball was hit your way or you stepped into the batter's box.

Even so, a highly developed memory is a competitive advantage for the human species. Memory is crucial to our survival, for it allows us to adapt and solve problems. I bet even Lasso has heard the adage that those who forget history are doomed to repeat it.

I write these thoughts on the first day of the new year. It is a new beginning. A clean slate. Perhaps you, gentle reader, would happily forget 2020. There have been many losses, tragedies and widespread suffering.

Yet, there are also lessons to remember.

Though the presidential election was bitterly contested, more Americans voted than ever before in history. Though the killings of George Floyd, Breonna Taylor and other Black Americans were brutal, more people have worked together to reform the injustices of systemic racism. Though quarantine and social distancing have kept people physically apart, more meetings and conversations have occurred through online platforms like Zoom video conferences.

OK, no one is saying Zoom is fun all the time! Still, many of us have come a long way with the technology.

Though we hope for healthier, happier times in 2021, we don't want to forget the ways that we've grown in response to these challenges, especially as COVID-19 mutates into new viral strands. Though a goldfish swims blissfully alone in the fishbowl, we cannot forget that we are in this world together.

While I think the metaphor about being a goldfish has its limitations, "Ted Lasso" is still the best show I've watched in the past year. This television coach understands the real-life truth that, whether the sport is American or English football, the essential lessons are the same: Great teams are built on mutual respect, cooperation and support. Teammates have to work hard on these relationships as well their individual skills like kicking or throwing a ball.

We are Republicans, Democrats and independents. We are different genders, races and ethnicities. We speak different languages and follow different religions. We like different sports!

But we must remember that we humans are on the same team.

Will We Choose Community or Chaos?

January 14, 2021

"Can anything good come out of Nazareth?"

This question was uttered in first-century Galilee (John 1:46), but I recognize the cynicism in our time and place.

Can anything good come out of Washington, D.C.?

Can anything good come out of Raleigh?

Can anything good come out of today's politics?

Next week, we remember the preacher, prophet and civil rights activist, Martin Luther King Jr., who is best known for his famous "I Have a Dream" speech. King asked many questions as well, particularly toward the end of his life.

In the last book he wrote before his assassination, King insisted, "We must not consider it unpatriotic to raise certain basic questions about our national character." He questioned white America's commitment to racial equity — why do so many say one thing, yet do another? He also lamented that so many citizens of the richest nation in human history still languished in poverty. He interrogated the reasons his country invested money and lives in the Vietnam War as well as called into question the morality of killing foreign citizens.

Despite his belief that such questions were necessary, King drew heavy criticism from even former supporters. But he did not probe the political realities of his time in order to sow seeds of cynicism or despair. He believed that our country faced an ultimate moral decision: to choose either community or chaos.

This same choice came to mind as I watched a mob storm the Capitol building in Washington on Jan. 6. I saw images of armed white supremacists and neo-Nazis. I saw images of the gallows that had been erected outside the building and pictures of Confederate flags waved inside our legislature.

Can anything good come out of this?

In the first century, there was a religious group known as Zealots who called for armed revolution. Their mission was to create chaos through a campaign of intimidation and violence.

Jesus specifically condemned such tactics, declaring that those who live by the sword shall die by the sword (Matthew 26:52).

At the same time that these zealots called for conflict and chaos, Jesus called for a new community — a community formed not by blood or birth, but by a command to love one another (John 13:34). For this reason, Martin Luther King Jr. called this movement "the beloved community" and extended it to all people of good faith in peacemaking.

King emphasized that the creation of this beloved community depended on nonviolent methods of civic action, including civil disobedience. It's not that historically oppressed people have no right to be upset. They should question the unjust authorities and work for societal change.

But King argued that the ends do not justify the means. While previous revolutions may have succeeded in creating change, they nevertheless resulted in bloodshed. The killing of innocents is never good. If America was to realize the cherished ideals of liberty and justice for all, it would not be at gunpoint.

The rioters in our nation's capital obviously believed otherwise, which raises the same fundamental question that King asked in his last book: "Where do we go from here? Community or chaos?" This remains a poignant question as our nation prepares for the presidential inauguration under the threat of more violence.

Yet, something good may come of this. We can choose the beloved community over violent chaos.

Our Consoler-in-Chief

January 21, 2021

President Joseph Biden has used his Constitutional authority to issue executive actions designed to revamp the federal response to the COVID-19 pandemic, bolster our nation's struggling economy, overhaul immigration legislation and restore international treaties to curb climate change.

Readers of the Chatham News + Record will have differing opinions about these actions, for they are in large part a repudiation of the previous administration's own executive orders.

But though there is disagreement about policy matters, I believe this president can inspire unity among residents of this land. Before his inauguration, Biden led a remembrance ceremony for the 400,000 Americans who have died from COVID-19.

He is our Consoler-in-Chief.

While Biden is not known for his oratorical brilliance, he is well-acquainted with grief. When he was only 30 years old, he lost his wife and daughter in a car accident the week before Christmas. Later in life, he lost another child to cancer.

Our president's history of personal tragedies allows him to speak directly and profoundly to our country's woes in the pandemic. While it was moving to see the luminaries dedicated to those who have died from COVID-19, Biden offered illuminating words as well: "To heal, we must remember."

Our larger culture expects us to move on quickly after our loved ones have died. Many people do not even say the word "dead" but use euphemisms like "passed away" or "gone home." It is painful to remember a loved one's death. But undertaker and poet Thomas

Lynch says that, even more than our fear of death, we fear that "our stories will die with us, and won't be told or will be told incorrectly."

We are most afraid we will be forgotten.

With this ultimate fear in mind, we should consider the connection our Consoler-in-Chief drew between healing and remembering. Perhaps lost in the sheer enormity of a number like 400,000 is that each death has ended a personal relationship — someone's son or daughter, mother or father, spouse, grandparent, neighbor or friend. Biden can relate to such heartbreaking loss. He sought to remember our nation's dead and thereby shine a light upon our collective grief. By acknowledging the pain, we may yet regroup and move forward together.

Biden directed those luminaries to be lit outside of the Lincoln Memorial, which is named for another president who oversaw another time in our nation's history of great suffering, loss and polarization. In our day, we must reunify our country after election controversy and the mob violence at the Capitol Building. Our nation is split along partisan lines as well as fractured by geographic, economic and racial differences.

Our Consoler-in-Chief understands the challenges we face. Once again, it is Biden's personal story that offers further illumination. And hope.

In 1977, he became engaged to Jill Jacobs. He wondered how she could agree to marry a man who admittedly was heartbroken over the death of his first wife. She replied, "Anybody who can love that deeply once can do it again."

Granted, a robust democracy is characterized by peaceful dissent. We will have our differences about policies and legislation. People will disagree with Biden's decisions. Like all of us, he will make mistakes.

Yet, his heart is in the right place. May the same be true of all of us who love our United States.

Velvet Hooks: Guys Hanging Out with Guys

February 4, 2021

I mentioned to my wife that my New Year's resolution was to hang out with more guy friends. She and I have two churches and three kids between us, so free time is rare. But she was immediately supportive: "You need that."

I knew two guys who played a weekly round of Frisbee or, more accurately, disc golf. I hadn't played since my undergraduate days, but this seemed like a good opportunity to spend time with them. When I wondered if I could tag along, they graciously agreed. I bought a couple of discs and met them at Rock Ridge Park just outside of Pittsboro.

This 18-hole course winding through the woods is a pleasure to walk, even on a gray morning in January. Most of my throws ended up among the trees and underbrush off the well-maintained path. We had no problem maintaining our social distance.

But we grew closer as friends.

There were no tearful confessions or dramatic declarations. But between the groans of wayward frisbees and the occasional hurrah of a well-thrown disc, we talked about stuff that matters: our families, childhoods and church.

After a few holes, I smiled and told them that I was enjoying this. I had just chucked yet another disc off a large oak, but they knew I wasn't talking about the game itself. I was hooked on hanging out together.

One of them shared that, on the drive to the park that very morning, he'd heard Billy Baker of the Boston Globe interviewed about his new memoir about friendships between guys. The book is titled "We Need to Hang Out." What a coincidence!

Baker's premise is that American men have difficulties building and maintaining friendships. Women talk face-to-face, but men talk shoulder-to-shoulder. In order to form bonds, men need a shared activity like ball golf or disc golf. Baker called this a "velvet hook" — something fun that makes a connection between people.

I played disc golf back in college but hanging out was never a problem in those days. There were intramural sports, parties and guys just lounging around the dorm playing video games like Mario Kart. Marriage, parenthood, career — what's popularly called "adulting" — have brought many beautiful and rewarding aspects to my life. But it's also true that now I need to make much more of an effort to hang out with other guys.

In the pandemic, any human connection is more complicated. But velvet hooks can be safe, especially if the activity is outside. Men can talk shoulder-to-shoulder if they wear facemasks and keep their distance. For only $20, you can buy a decent set of discs. And it's free to play at Rock Ridge Park — a local treasure for friends to share.

I played nine holes that morning before I needed to get back home to the laptop, cell phone and family. In the parking lot, I made a joke that I'd love to play next week, if I could still move my throwing arm!

But I'd already resolved to play again with them. Even if my arm was so sore that I had to throw left-handed.

Tell Me, Tell Me

February 11, 2021

Our firstborn was only 3 years old and happily racing toy cars across our front porch when he received his first bee sting. His mother rocked him in her lap until he had calmed down. Then, in her wisdom, she told him the story of her first sting as a little girl when she had walked barefoot in the backyard grass.

For months afterward, our son would ask friends and strangers, "Have you been stung by a bee? Tell me about when you got it."

It is hard for me to wrap my head around the 26.9 million people infected with the coronavirus in the United States. The 791,000 in North Carolina is overwhelming enough.

But I know the stories of friends, family and parishioners who got it. The rattling, aching cough. The muscles spasms traveling from the neck down to the feet. The dizziness at the slightest physical effort. Feeling like they had been run over by a truck or train. The fear that they would get worse.

I also hear stories from people who have gotten either one or both COVID-19 vaccinations. Many of them report no difficulties. Some experience soreness in their arms. A few have had flu-like symptoms for 24 to 48 hours such as a low-grade fever, muscle aches and fatigue.

But no one has ever told me that suffering the vaccine is as terrible as the actual coronavirus. It seems obvious that everyone should be vaccinated as soon as possible.

But last week, I was part of a video conference call led by Dr. Sharon Reilly, the medical director of Piedmont Health. She called out myths that are circulating in our community and nationwide: that the vaccine will alter your DNA and that the shot introduces a tracer microchip into your body.

I cannot take such ridiculous and debunked conspiracy theories seriously; however, the consequences of such misinformation are deadly serious. If the coronavirus remains active, infecting non-vaccinated people, the chances increase that it will mutate, possibly into forms that resist the vaccine. These new strains of COVID-19 could be even more deadly.

Why do these conspiracy theories about the vaccine and the virus itself remain active among a significant percentage of our population?

I can't help but wonder how many of those who believe this misinformation have actually known someone who has suffered or died from the infection. This is the reason why I began with bee stings and stories.

Tell me about when you got it. My young son learned that asking for a story can open up a conversation with a complete stranger. Granted, a child's innocence encourages many of us to lower our defenses. But a story has the power to create empathy and unite the storyteller with the listener.

It is this power of story that causes me to believe that stories are prayers. A genuine curiosity about someone's experience with COVID-19 not only implies that you take the virus seriously, but that you take that particular person seriously — you value that individual's experience. If we seek the stories of our friends, neighbors and even strangers, we will feel less alone and perhaps less afraid. We will be less likely to believe conspiracy theories and more likely to care for one another.

Tell me about when you got it. And I shall listen while silently giving thanks that we are together.

To Clean Our House, We Must Name the Mess

February 18, 2021

Only seven Republican senators voted to convict former President Donald Trump for inciting the mob attack on our Capitol building Jan. 6. Yet, there is widespread disapproval of the rioters.

The violence on that day was appalling. At least 140 police officers and security guards were injured. Those men and women were beaten and bloodied, pepper-sprayed and trampled. Their fingers were snapped, their eyes gouged, and they suffered heart attacks as a result of repeated tasing by rioters. Five people died, including one security guard. And the insurrectionists intended more bloodshed, even the assassination of elected officials like Vice President Mike Pence.

Numerous photos and videos documented rioters waving Confederate flags, brandishing neo-Nazi insignia and yelling racial slurs. Despite this clear evidence that groups were affiliated with white supremacist and nationalist groups, some Americans still believe the false claim that the attack was carried out by members of leftist groups like antifa — meaning "antifascist," a term that describes far-left-leaning militant groups.

Let the record show: The arrests of actual rioters have linked these individuals to far-right groups such as the Three Percenters, the Oath Keepers and the Proud Boys. Those who attacked our fellow citizens and threatened our very democratic process were homegrown terrorists. We must condemn not only the attack but the toxic ideology of white supremacy that motivated them.

Long ago, Jesus of Nazareth said that the truth would set us free (John 8:32). I am reminded of how this same rabbi compared a person's inner life — thoughts and motivations — to a house (Matthew 12:43–45; Luke 11:24–26). The metaphor holds that an "unclean spirit" may be removed from a house as if taking out the trash. But Jesus added that each of us must remain vigilant after the initial spring cleaning, for that same unclean spirit will return with more spirits. If they find the house neat and in a good order, they will cause even more disarray than the original mess!

It is true that Americans have addressed injustices in our past. In the 150 years since the Civil War, we have abolished slavery and legislated equal rights. Trailblazing men and women of color have integrated nearly every aspect of our common life, contributing to the general welfare with their genius and talent as well as raising their own stations in life.

But on Jan. 6, we witnessed a racist mob invade our Capitol. They more than made a mess of things. There was blood on the floor. In this case, the unclean spirit was white supremacy. This hateful ideology has come back with a vengeance, and it is the responsibility of every person who calls this nation home to name and denounce this evil that has arisen in our midst.

In modern culture, we do not think of unclean spirits in the same way our ancestors did. Yet, ancient advice remains relevant. We must remain vigilant about cleaning out malevolent ideologies.

The truth is racism is not a thing of the distant past. We are neither a post-racial nor colorblind society. Such falsehoods, even if they are well-intentioned, still prevent us from recognizing the real and present threat of white supremacist terrorists.

As we witnessed Jan. 6, we avoid the truth at the peril of our national soul.

When Chickens Roost, No Red Herrings

February 25, 2021

After the terrible winter storms last week, we saw image after image of human misery in Texas. Millions were forced to endure freezing temperatures without electrical power not only because of the ice and snow but also the weakness in the power grid.

The state's electric grid operator, the Electric Reliability Council of Texas, intentionally shut off power in a series of rolling blackouts. Officials had to take these extreme measures to prevent a statewide collapse of the entire system.

Tensions among Texans ran high. There were reports that citizens harassed power line crews in Austin and San Antonio, even throwing things at workers. While anger is understandable, it is completely misdirected at the employees fixing the downed power lines.

Texans should take their anger right to the top of their political system.

Reliability council officials and Texas lawmakers had no excuse. A winter storm in February 2011 also resulted in widespread blackouts. Officials knew their equipment would not perform in extremely cold temperatures. Still, they did little to upgrade those systems.

Now the chickens have come home to roost as past failures have resulted in today's problems.

Under intense scrutiny, Gov. Greg Abbott blamed the failure on the state's renewable energy systems, such as wind turbines, despite the fact that such energy sources contribute only a small fraction of the power supply to the state. As reported by the USA Today, Daniel Cohan, an associate professor of civil and environmental engineering at Rice University, noted that the combination of natural gas, coal and nuclear power plants failed to meet the consumer demand. Cohen labeled Abbott's argument about the wind turbines "a red herring" — an intentionally misleading statement.

When confronted with the facts, Abbott tried an even more desperate smoke screen, blaming Rep. Alexandria Ocasio-Cortez for a plan called the Green New Deal. Please bear in mind this congresswoman represents the state of New York, not Texas, and that no such federal legislation has even been proposed.

Why attack renewable energy sources? In the same USA Today article, Emily Grubert, an assistant professor of civil and environmental engineering at Georgia Institute of Technology, made a wise observation: "It's easy to focus on the thing that you can see changing as the source of why an outcome is changing." In this case, easy to blame wind turbines (and the political party that advocated for them) as the cause of failures in the power supply.

The truth is that the Texan leaders who did not sufficiently upgrade and maintain the power plants are at fault. But the more pressing and fundamental issue is that cheap fossil fuels are part of the problem.

Instead of excuses and political jabs, all elected officials must take seriously the predictions of more frequent and serious storms due to climate change. Since renewable energy sources help to decrease carbon emissions, these forms of energy are exactly the types of technologies we need.

Proponents of natural gas, coal and oil are right about one thing. The investment in new sources of energy will take time and money.

But to continue to rely on fossil fuels will prove even more than costly. It will be deadly.

The United States must launch a broad bipartisan effort to act now in order to improve and expand our energy capabilities with wind, water and solar. Then, we will be better able to withstand storms and prevent more disastrous weather. The chickens have come home to roost. We cannot afford to waste time with red herrings.

Facing the COVID Death Count

March 4, 2021

It is almost spring. The signs are all around us. Nature is greening again. The chorus of birds has returned to the trees. The days grow longer, and just yesterday I saw my first daffodil offer its yellow smile.

For Christians, this is the liturgical season of Lent, a word derived from Old English that originally referred to spring. The paradox is, despite the signs of new life in nature that are all around us, Christians have traditionally used Lent as a time to focus on death.

Lent begins on Ash Wednesday when worshippers receive the mark of the cross in ash on their foreheads. This is to remind us not only of the universal truth of mortality but also that it is personal. Everyone is mortal. I will die. Remembering my mortality can make me thankful for life today.

Even if they have never heard of ashes, people of different faiths may still be familiar with the popular Christian practice of "giving something up" during Lent. Maybe chocolate, wine or reality TV shows. This Lent, my 8-year-old son wanted our family to give up eating meat. The point again relates to raising awareness. Giving something up can result in gratitude for what we have.

In addition to going vegetarian, I have added something I consider to be a spiritual practice. Every day I learn the story of a fellow North Carolinian who has died of COVID-19.

Over the past few days, I've read of Tar Heel State natives who traveled the globe and others who were born and died in the same county. I've read about decorated war heroes and accomplished professionals. Politicians, factory workers, preachers and teachers. Mountain mamas and country gentlemen. Folks who had lived through the Great Depression, Jim Crow and 9/11. An immigrant who became a sheriff's deputy. A survivor of Hodgkin's lymphoma who became a nurse.

Loved ones remembered their deceased with stories: He had witnessed the explosion of the first atomic bomb. She loved Cajun cooking, especially jambalaya. Another remembered her as "a fighter" and him as a "bright presence." A son said his dad had never met a stranger, and even his bank teller cried at the news of his death.

These are just a few of the more than 11,000 dead from COVID-19 in North Carolina who are part of 500,000 people in this country alone linked by cause of death. I cannot imagine 500,000 of anything, let alone the magnitude of such suffering and loss.

But these stories give life to the statistics. Stories inspire the living.

Despite the vastly different life experiences of their loved ones, I've noticed a common theme: Many relatives and friends wish to carry on the legacy of the person who died. Time and time again, people shared that they wanted to be as good a provider or as good a parent. To be as kind and loyal, generous and loving.

Receiving the cross on my forehead this Ash Wednesday was particularly poignant. This Lent has been marked by death as never before in my lifetime. Though I have not lost a loved one to the coronavirus, my daily Lenten practice has put faces on the death count. Not everyone believes the Christian claim that life springs from death. But I think we can agree that the memory of the dead can inspire the living.

Wearing Masks Should Not Be a Question

March 11, 2021

Last week, members of the clergy were authorized to receive the COVID-19 vaccine as part of "Group 3 Frontline Essential Workers." With a spring in my step, I entered the UNC-Chapel Hill Friday Center wearing a facemask and a Carolina baseball cap. I was so excited that I momentarily blanked when asked for my birthdate.

"Sweetie," the nurse smiled, "it's not a trick question."

As she readied the needle, she complimented my choice of baseball cap. She told me that, though she had attended East Carolina University, she had married a Tar Heel. I started to say that I had likewise "married up" when, suddenly, my shot was over! It was painless.

As she put an adhesive bandage on my shoulder, the nurse instructed me to keep practicing the three w's to minimize the risk of COVID-19 exposure and spread: wash my hands, wait six feet apart, and — most importantly — wear a mask.

I lamented that day's news that both Texas and Mississippi had lifted their mask mandates.

The nurse shook her head. "I don't get it. Why spend a whole year building a house and burn it down at the very end?"

After a full year of the COVID-19 pandemic, there are signs that the end is in sight. There are three safe, effective vaccines. As was true with my experience in Chapel Hill, there are countless dedicated workers and volunteers getting these shots into people's arms.

Now is the time to be vaccinated as soon as we are able.

While waiting for everyone to have the opportunity to receive this miracle of modern medicine, we must do everything we can to prevent the spread of infection. The science is clear that facemasks do exactly that.

Yet, there are now 15 states without mask mandates. Why are they willing to risk fanning the COVID-19 flames right when the fire finally seems to be under control?

Mississippi Gov. Tate Reeves, a Republican, justified his decision: "The governor's office is getting out of the business of telling people what they can and cannot do." I realize that's a talking point for his political party. There is a time and place for competition in the political area as opposing ideologies duke it out in the court of public opinion.

But public health is neither a game nor a partisan issue.

Mask mandates do not represent an overreach of government authority; they are not a violation of individual rights. They are a responsibility to the larger public.

I would remind Reeves, a self-proclaimed advocate for law and order, of the words found on the side of most police cars: "Serve and Protect." Mask mandates serve the best interests of the larger community by helping create herd immunity. Masks also protect individuals from this deadly virus.

The mask mandate has been extended in the Tar Heel State until at least March 26 by Democratic Gov. Roy Cooper. Similar extensions have also been made by Republican governors in West Virginia, Utah, Ohio, Indiana, Maryland and Massachusetts.

In the deeply red state of Alabama, Gov. Kay Ivey extended the mask mandate until April 9. Governor Mee-Maw, as the 76-year-old politician is known, told her constituents, "I'm just trying to urge you to use the common sense the good Lord gave each of us to be smart and considerate of others."

While I know the nurse, who administered my vaccine shared my college basketball preference, I do not know her religious or political affiliation. But I feel confident that she would join me in responding to Ivey with a hearty Amen.

Moments to Live by in the Year of the Pandemic

March 18, 2021

When the pandemic began one year ago, I started eating a handful of M&M's every day after lunch. I've never had much of a craving for desserts, but now I look forward to this daily taste of sweetness.

Throughout the pandemic, my wife and I have danced after supper with our three young children. Last summer, we had a phase when we boogied to the soundtrack of the musical "Hamilton." But our children have returned to their favorite superhero theme songs: the "Superman" movie score by John Williams and the opening tune from the "Batman" TV show starring Adam West. Listening to those songs for the umpteenth time, I admit I was sometimes impatient to start the bedtime routine of bath and books.

But other nights have been so fun I've lost track of the hour. The way the kids help me stay in the moment is their superpower.

The church that I serve as pastor has developed new habits and routines in the pandemic as well. In addition to the online and outdoor worship services, we started a weekly prayer meeting with another congregation. In the beginning, everyone dialed into a conference call. Now, we meet every Sunday afternoon on a Zoom video conference.

Our members are white; theirs are Black. The impetus for this ministry was last summer's death of George Floyd under the knee of the white police officer. I am under no illusions that we or any other white people are saviors.

But I speak for many in our church when I say that we have been blessed by the faith of our Black friends.

One of their deacons opens our meeting with a hymn. He starts off almost in a whisper, then grows louder and stronger in his gravely baritone. This gentleman often sings spirituals like "Swing Low, Sweet Chariot," "Go Down, Moses," and "Steal Away to Jesus." These words and melodies have given Black people strength to endure and resist evils from the time of slavery down to the present reality of police brutality. This is the genius of the Black church. Writer Zora Neale Hurston once called such faith "an inside thing to live by."

Recently, this faithful deacon belted out, "Count your blessings. Name them one by one." When he had finished, the rest of us took turns sharing examples of unexpected grace that had come out of this pandemic, including the friendships made between our churches. We try to keep our meetings under an hour, but in listening to everyone's blessings, I once again lost track of time.

By sharing these stories, I do not intend to diminish anyone's suffering during the COVID-19 pandemic. I realize many have faced economic hardships and lost loved ones to this terrible disease. Many of my own family members, friends and parishioners have been stressed, anxious or lonely. I would never tell someone in pain or grief to "count your blessings" or put on a happy face.

I share my stories to offer a little taste of what has helped me through these times. I have one more story:

During the pandemic, the creek that runs through the woods behind my neighborhood has been my family's refuge. Several years ago, a large oak fell across the water from one side of the bank to the other. I have often sat on the fallen trunk, legs dangling over the creek, watching my kids play along the bank or in the water.

There have been plenty of times when I fretted about my to-do list. But other times, I have breathed slowly. And given thanks.

I hope we cross to the other side of this pandemic. As we journey ahead, I hope each of us finds our own "inside things to live by" — music that moves us, quiet places that still us, love that comforts and inspires us.

Just a little taste of sweetness can fill us with gratitude.

Afterword: Churchless Sermon for Easter

I am a Christian pastor and a believer in the Resurrection. I capitalize "Resurrection" in reference to the faith of the church that a man named Jesus was raised from the dead.

For this churchless sermon, intended for readers who do not necessarily share my faith or tradition, I use lowercase "resurrection" not in a dismissive or pejorative way, but to indicate the general sense of the word — a resurrection means "to rise again" and can refer to many different things or events.

This is the season of Easter, but resurrections occur all the time. Think of the rising of the sun as the resurrection of the day. Think of the resurrections during the spring season — greening trees and blooming flowers after the cold, bare winter.

Again, I do not write to discredit such resurrections. They may even save lives.

That's why, when I want to hear a resurrection sermon, I listen to addicts.

I know people, blessed and broken like all of us, who display the rare courage to talk about death and their own death-dealing impulses — their bents for self-destructiveness, shame spirals and cavernous holes of regret. It is only by naming such chasms that they believe they can keep from falling back into them. Alcoholics Anonymous claims, "We must face who we are, else we die."

It is also true the first steps of AA are to admit powerlessness over addiction and believe that a Higher Power brings recovery from addiction and resurrection to new life. Likewise, the New Testament is clear that the Resurrection of Jesus was an act by a Higher Power — a force greater than nature. Humans cannot bring life from death

117

any more than we can spin the Earth through space and recreate spring.

But it is clear to me from listening to addicts preach that resurrections still require human effort. That is a lesson for all of us.

This Easter, I have heard many people hoping for a return to "normal" after the COVID-19 pandemic. Next year, I hope it will be safe to gather in churches for Sunday worship.

It is also clear that the world outside the walls of our sanctuaries needs our attention. We need to face some painful truths about what is "normal" in our community.

In the fall of 2020, the Chatham County Public Health Department released a study of "health disparities" — preventable differences in health outcomes between groups in our society. Disparities occur across many dimensions, including race/ethnicity, socioeconomic status, age, location, gender, disability status and sexual orientation. Even before the coronavirus, "normal" was often unjust and inequitable.

Like any addict, the society that has created and perpetuated these "disparities" must first face the truth about itself. We cannot return to the status quo or business as usual. Once we name the injustices and inequalities, we must rise up to transform them.

I wrap up this churchless sermon by noting that writer Flannery O'Connor claimed, "everything that rises must converge." May people of all faiths work together to address disparities and bring about a new day for justice and equality. May it be so: amen.

Photo by Ginny Taylor-Troutman, 2021.

CPSIA information can be obtained
at www.ICGtesting.com
Printed in the USA
FSHW022318270521
81749FS